Family Matters

DISCOVERING THE MENNONITE BRETHREN

Family Matters

DISCOVERING THE MENNONITE BRETHREN

Lynn Jost and Connie Faber

WINNIPEG, MANITOBA   HILLSBORO, KANSAS

Published simultaneously by Kindred Productions, Winnipeg, Manitoba R2L 2E5 and Kindred Productions, Hillsboro, Kansas 67063

We wish to acknowledge the contribution of Katie Funk Wiebe to this volume. Her original book *Who are the Mennonite Brethren?* served as a source of information, wording and ideas.

Thanks to Tabor College for providing sabbatical release for Lynn Jost to work on this book.

The photo for the Part Two sectional page is courtesy of the Centre for Mennonite Brethren Studies, Winnipeg, Manitoba.

Cover and Book Design: Armadillo Design
Printed by The Christian Press

National Library of Canada Cataloguing in Publication Data

Jost, Lynn, 1954-
    Family matters

ISBN 0-921788-74-6

1. Mennonite Brethren Church. I. Faber, Connie, 1957- II. Title.
BX8129.M373J67 2002   289.7   C2002-910391-6

International Standard Book Number: 0-921788-74-6

Introduction

The name Mennonite Brethren may suggest the defining essence, the identifying metaphor, of the denomination. We are family. Whether we like the name or not, Mennonite Brethren says a lot about who we are. We are, or we aim to be, God's family. We are sisters and brothers in Christ. This notion, "Church is family," is the Mennonite Brethren gift for postmodern North American Christian identity.

In the book, *Families at the Crossroads*, Rodney Clapp reminds us that the church is God's family. The church family is God's most important institution on earth. The church is the foremost social agent. The church family shapes Christian character. The church is the means for God to save a waiting, desperate world.

This is the confession of Mennonite Brethren. The church most clearly defines our identity. While we may protest that this ideal is not a reality in many MB congregations, the purpose of this book is not simply to report what is. It is a call to remember what has been and to return to what should be and will be.

The church is our primary home. As Anabaptists, we begin reading the Bible not with the creation account in the first chapter of Genesis but with the story of Jesus in the Gospels. There we see that Jesus claims that his primary family relationship is with those who do God's will, who live out the reign of God (Mark 3:31-35). "Whoever does the will of God is my brother and sister and mother," he said (v. 35).

Jesus' notion of family grew out of his Hebrew understanding of covenant. At its core, the covenant was a family relationship. God promised Abram a family that would become a nation. Marriage and family were at the essence of Israel's identity and purpose. But it was not until the exodus from Egypt that Israel became a nation, a mature covenant community. As Exodus 12:38 tells us, the covenant nation was "a mixed multitude," not a blood kinship that was set apart from its neighbors ethnically. Although Israel had ties to biological family, at its core the meaning of Israel was a people of God, because of God's historical acts. By insisting on a family based on ethics not ethnicity, Jesus was consistent with the covenant God made with Israel in the Hebrew Bible.

Jesus called the disciples to join the community of God's reign. Jesus united the world's divided communities into a single new humanity (Eph. 2:11-22). In Christ Jesus, states Ephesians 2:19, "you are fellow citizens... you are of God's household." The call to faith, to following Jesus, is a call to become part of the family of God.

Jesus gives identity particularly to those who are marginalized, to those who have no family. In the Old Testament, God explicitly includes marginal people like orphans, widows and foreigners in the covenant people. In the new covenant, Jesus announces good news for the poor, the lame, the blind, the prisoner. The family of God is composed of the lost, the last, the least, the little and the dead (Capon, *The Parables of Grace*). Biological connections are incidental not programmatic.

Paul reiterates this theme. To join Christ, Paul says, is to join God's family. He uses many metaphors to describe the church, but perhaps his most significant is the family. He uses the phrase "my brothers (and sisters)" more than 65 times in his letters. The early church met in household groups. Baptism was admitting newly adopted children into God's family. The Lord's Supper recalled a daily family activity. When Acts 16:31 includes the house in the salvation call, "you and your household shall be saved," we should think of the entire household of slaves rather than the biological family of the Philippian jailer. The primary kinship links for Paul were those of the family of God.

The "church as family" metaphor offers a number of practical links in telling the story of who we are. The circumstances of our beginnings, in a renewal sprung from an emphasis on an intimate relationship with Jesus and fostered in intimate group Bible study and prayer, birthed in us a family feeling. The conflict and difficulties inherent in the founding, which involved a break with the existing Mennonite church, further strengthened the need to rely on and be "family" for one another.

Perhaps no application of the metaphor is more central to the Mennonite Brethren story, however, than the notion of strangers and aliens. As mentioned above, the Hebrew Bible gives privileged place to aliens or foreigners. The historical and theological basis for this special status is the origin of Israel itself. Israel began as a nation of strangers. Outsiders. Because they were aliens in Egypt, Israel is called to provide for strangers (Lev. 19:33-34; Exod. 23:9; Deut. 10:17-19). Jesus himself was a homeless person with no place to "lay his head" (Matt. 8:20). Repeatedly, the New Testament calls Christians to welcome strangers into their homes. Christians practice hospitality.

Like Israel, MBs began from a common biological stock. All of the charter MBs came from German-speaking Mennonite colonies in Russia. They or their forebearers had been migrants from Prussia and, before that, from Holland. Within two decades of the origin of the MB Church, Mennonites began migrating as strangers to North America.

Immediately upon birth in Russia, the desire was wakened to reach out and welcome strangers into the family, whether these be the Slavic people in the area or people in the mission field of India or Congo. Ironically, our story also reveals that, like the New Testament church, we have often resisted or moved too slowly in including new ethnicities within our congregations. Nevertheless, this exciting interplay of being family, being strangers on a pilgrimage, and welcoming new family members has characterized the Mennonite Brethren Church throughout its history.

Getting to know a family well involves the discovery of its particular and current traits, and it also involves studying its background. The first task identifies those characteristics and views that we might call the family's particular "ethos," and identifies its passion and resources. The second offers some explanation of why things are the way they are.

But does one begin with the present or the past? In this book, we begin with the origins of the Mennonite Brethren Church (briefly tracing our roots back into church history as well), and then discuss our theological distinctives. We conclude with a look at our growth in North America, some of our institutions and the worldwide MB family. The story could easily be read in a different order, however, perhaps by beginning with our distinctives and then the historical sketch. You are invited to consult the Contents page and enjoy the book the way you prefer.

Above all, welcome!

PART ONE

Family
History

Chapter 1
The Anabaptist Reformation

Early Church

New beginnings create thrills. A wedding. A newborn baby. Above all, a new church plant. In each case, we experience the joy of a new family begun. Acts 1 to 8 tells the exciting story of the birth of Christ's family, the church. Jesus' followers, discouraged and huddled behind locked doors, were transformed. They saw the risen Lord. At Pentecost, they were powerfully anointed by God with the Holy *Spirit*.

The newly established church became courageous, defying opposition and persecution. "Jesus reigns!" they proclaimed. "Jesus is Lord!" they declared. Such assertions, such allegiances clearly challenged the political power structures of Jerusalem and subsequently Rome. If Jesus was Lord, then Caesar was not. Evangelism was met by persecution, and even martyrdom, but the blood of the martyrs became the seed of the church.

The new reign of God transformed the daily lives of those who joined it. Christians lived as a new family. They worshiped together, ate together, shared belongings with those in need. They studied the Scriptures, excitedly discovering that the Old Testament was being fulfilled with their response to Jesus, the Messiah. They wanted to live new and holy lives, so accepted the discipline of the church. They discovered that love for God produced a radical love within them, not only for the Christian family but for the others around them.

As Christians witnessed to the power of God, the church spread from Jerusalem to all the regions around the Mediterranean basin. Persecutors hunted and killed Christians, acting—they thought—to defend God and country. Under pressure, some turned away from following Jesus. Many, however, remained firm in their convictions. For every Christian who became discouraged and fell away, many others converted to the One who could give to his followers such courage.

Constantine and Catholicism

By 320 C.E. the church had become so popular that the Emperor Constantine converted to Christianity, making it not only legal but protected. Hierarchy and sacramentalism had already been creeping into church life. Now the temptation to use force to defend the faith brought about what Mennonites later called "the fall of the church."

Despite commitment to pass along traditions of the Christian faith, creedalism replaced spiritual vigor. The family of Christ became an institution vying for power and prestige. Abuses of religious power grew increasingly menacing during the Middle Ages. The powerful state church gained enormous wealth by selling indulgences (licenses to sin) and demanding payment to release loved ones from purgatory. Pilgrimages to the Holy Land produced strife in the name of the Prince of Peace. The Mass was distorted from a celebration of Christ's victory on the cross to a re-offering of his body to gain God's favor. Relics of saints promised supernatural power. Money-hungry, immoral popes lived like kings instead of serving the King of kings. The church had lost her vitality.

Protestant Reformation

Enter Martin Luther. The German priest began studying the New Testament, especially Paul's letter to the Romans. He became convinced God offered the divine gift of righteousness to believing children of God. By faith, Luther experienced new birth in Christ.

In 1517, Luther became deeply troubled over the selling of indulgences. Unable to convince his archbishop to support internal reform, he went public with 95 theses or statements, which were indictments of church abuses. Controversy flared. Luther had kindled a fire that would not go out.

Luther began to teach that salvation was a gift from God to be received by faith. He maintained that the Bible, not the Pope, was God's authority on earth. Purgatory, indulgences, relics, the sacrificial Mass and prayers to the saints were churchly traditions, not biblical truth.

In Switzerland, two other reformers reached similar conclusions. In Geneva, John Calvin, a former lawyer, succeeded in a manner much like Luther's. Like Luther, he rejected Catholicism and he wrote extensively, developing a thorough theological system. Like Luther, he also retained the practice of a state church. In Switzerland, as in Germany and the Catholic lands, the ruling prince determined church identity. In the lands of a Lutheran prince, the church christened Lutheran babies. In the Reformed Swiss cantons, babies were baptized into the Reformed church.

The other Swiss reformer was Ulrich Zwingli of Zurich. Known as the "People's Priest," Zwingli was flamboyant, energetic and a powerful preacher. He preached exegetically—verse by verse, chapter by chapter.

Like his fellow reformers, Zwingli's study of the Bible led him to recognize the abuses of the Catholic Church. With the approval of the city council, he pushed aside one Catholic practice after another. In 1525, six years after he had begun his ministry, Zwingli led a biblical observance of the Lord's Supper. Unlike the Catholics who taught that the wafer of the Mass became Christ's physical body and blood, and unlike Luther who held that the bread and wine became the "real presence" of Christ, Zwingli saw the Lord's Supper as a memorial. He emphasized Jesus' words, "Do this in memory of me." Zwingli also taught that the church and its services should be free of ostentation. The church service was a place for hearing and teaching the Word of God.

Radical Reformation

Through his visionary ministry Zwingli attracted a group of young radicals who wanted even more radical reform of church life. Conrad Grebel, a bright but rebellious son of high society whose decadent life had been transformed through new birth in Christ, and his colleague Felix Manz, broke with Zwingli on the issue of baptism. Following the counsel of civil authorities,

Zwingli had continued the practice of infant baptism. Grebel, insisting that the state had nothing to do with church practice, argued for believers' baptism.

Under the question of baptism was a deeper issue dividing Zwingli and Grebel: the nature of the church. Was it to be a state church, in which all citizens of a region are also church members, or a believers' church, in which only persons who repent of sin, turn to Christ and give total loyalty to Jesus are baptized?

When the Zurich Council ordered Grebel and Manz to stop their home Bible studies, the break was complete. On January 21, 1525, this group met to pray about their critical situation. Moved by the Spirit and with great fear, every person present was baptized and pledged to live in separation from the world. Anabaptism—to be baptized again—was born.

The Brethren, as they called themselves, witnessed to their faith with joy and great courage. Grebel's evangelistic preaching brought hundreds of converts to know the Lord. Grebel was frequently imprisoned and his health failed; he died of the plague in the summer of 1526.

Manz, too, though in and out of jail, evangelized and baptized new converts. On January 5, 1527, Manz became the first martyr of the Anabaptists. Sentenced to be drowned, Manz sang from the boat on his way to his death. His final words became a hymn calling for faithfulness in persecution.

The theology of the early Anabaptists, like that of the New Testament church, was developed "on the run," and much of what we know about it is from the court records of their enemies. A South German convert, Michael Sattler, however, wrote out the basic theology of the Swiss Anabaptists as agreed to at a conference held in the Swiss village of Schleitheim on February 24, 1527. It said:

1. Only believers who give evidence of transformed lives shall be baptized.
2. Those who return to a life of sin and refuse to return to faithful discipleship are to be banned from the church.
3. Believers must be united in faith and believers' baptism before taking the Lord's Supper.

4. Christians must live a holy life separated from the surrounding sinful society. The congregation is served by pastors who preach the Word, preside at the Lord's Supper, and provide pastoral oversight to the members.
5. Christians take the attitude of the suffering Christ and renounce force, violence and warfare.
6. Members follow the teachings of Christ in the Sermon on the Mount and refuse to take oaths, even the civil oath, but instead affirm the truth.

Sattler lived less than three months after the Schleitheim conference. He was convicted on the grounds of the confessional statement he had helped shape. His tongue was cut off, his body repeatedly pierced with hot tongs, and he was burned at the stake. The stories of Sattler and many other Anabaptist men and women who died for their beliefs have been recorded in the *Martyr's Mirror*. The record includes not only men but also many women who died for their faith. One such mother of faith was Machen Wens who died in Antwerp in October of 1573. Wens, the wife of a minister and mother of five, resisted months of torture but refused to recant her Anabaptist evangelical faith. Because of her powerful witness, the court insisted that her tongue be fastened with a screw to silence her witness before she went to be burned at the stake. Her oldest son, Adrian Wens, age 15, brought his youngest brother Hans, age 3, to witness the execution. Adrian fainted when the torch was put to his mother's body, but when he came to, he searched the ashes for the tongue screw as a memory. A letter she wrote on the eve of her death to young Adrian has been preserved. She wrote:

My dear son, I hope now to go before you; follow me as much as you value your soul. I now commend you to the Lord. Love one another all your days; take little Hans on your arm now and then for me. If your father should be taken from you, care for one another. The Lord keep you one and all. My dear children, kiss one another once for me, for remembrance. Adieu, my dear children, adieu.

7

Menno Simons

The Swiss Anabaptists were fervent missionaries throughout southern Europe. Eventually, their teachings were also carried north to Holland, where the brothers Obbe and Dirk Philips became early leaders of the church. They held to believers' baptism, nonviolent resistance to evil, and a call to a disciplined church. It was another Dutch Anabaptist leader, Menno Simons, however, who gave his name to the Mennonite Church.

Born in Holland in 1496, Menno became a Catholic priest. He was a typical priest of the time, performing the formal religious rituals but otherwise occupying himself with card playing, drinking and frivolity. Three factors jolted Menno Simons out of his spiritual stupor and into leadership in the Radical Reformation.

The first was in 1525, during his first year as priest, when Menno began having doubts about the dogma of transubstantiation. As he was celebrating the mass, a doubt struck him: are the bread and wine actually miraculously changed into the flesh and blood of Christ? In his struggle with this question, Menno did something that would radically change his life. He began a thorough search of the New Testament. He discovered that the Scriptures did not support many of the Catholic understandings he had been teaching. Menno was forced to make a choice: was his authority the church or the Bible?

Second, Menno was shocked into reconsidering his commitment to the Catholic priesthood by the news that a simple tailor, Sicke Freerks Snijder, had been beheaded because of his rebaptism on March 20, 1531. Though Menno had read some writings that advocated the principle of liberty regarding the age of baptism, he was stunned to learn that the simple, pious Freerks believed the Scriptures taught baptism as an adult confession of personal faith. Turning again to the New Testament, Menno concluded that infant baptism had no scriptural basis. He also found that the retention of infant baptism by the mainline Protestant reformers was not based on the Word of God but on human reason.

At this point, in 1531, Menno was convinced that the Anabaptists were correct regarding three truths: that the Bible, and not church tradition, was the authority in matters of faith; that the Lord's Supper was a memorial commemorating Christ's redemptive act, not a sacrifice of his flesh and blood; that baptism was an act of faithful adult discipleship, not a christening event to make children Christians. Yet he stayed in his priestly office. A third shock moved Menno from thought to action. A group of radical Anabaptist peasants got involved in a violent attempt to overthrow the dominant upper class at Muenster in northwest Germany. Some of the people in Menno's parish, the very ones most influenced by his radical teaching, were swept away with revolutionary zeal. When his own brother was killed in revolutionary battle, Menno could no longer remain silent. From the first, he had vigorously opposed the Muensterite error. Now Menno felt that their blood was upon his soul. The event moved Menno Simons to preach his new ideas openly, beginning in April 1535. By January of 1536 Menno publicly renounced the Catholic Church and withdrew to study and write in Groningen in northeast Holland.

Menno's retreat was broken by a visit from a group of believers begging him to accept ordination as an elder of the Anabaptists. Menno resisted, asking for time to pray and consider the call. After an intense struggle, Menno yielded and in 1537 was ordained an elder by Obbe Philips. No one knows exactly when Menno was rebaptized.

The group desperately needed a strong leader. Many had joined the Anabaptist revolutionaries and been slaughtered in war. Some had fled persecution, abandoning the church. The remaining evangelical faithful were discouraged, scattered and dwindling. Menno gave himself to the role of overseer of the congregations in Holland (1536-43), northwest Germany (1543-46), and Holstein under Danish rule (1546-61). In 1536 Menno married Gertrude, a godly woman who bore him several children, but he maintained no permanent residence. He traveled to visit the scattered brothers and sisters, preaching, baptizing, evangelizing, building up the church.

Menno was a hunted man. A price of 100 gold guilders was placed on his head in 1542. One man he had baptized in West Friesland was executed because he had sheltered Menno. Others baptized by Menno were also martyred.

Menno himself seemed to stay a step ahead of his persecutors. During these years he wrote about two dozen books and pamphlets. His writings helped establish and hold together the scattered, confused, persecuted church. His writings contain substantial doctrinal expositions of repentance, faith, the new birth and holiness. Written for the common person, his books became even more popular when authorities banned them.

Menno Simons was not the founder of the Mennonites. The church bears his name, however, for good reasons. He was a church leader who rallied a scattered people and led them through a time of great tribulation. His character encouraged the persecuted church, for he lived with "deep conviction, unshakable devotion, fearless courage, and calm trust" (Bender, 29). And, Menno was a New Testament theologian. For him the Bible was the sole authority in matters of faith and life.

For Menno, Christianity involved both faith and obedience. The Christian was called to live in the way of Christ. Menno's writings focus a clear vision of twin biblical ideals: practical holiness and the free church. The way of Christ involves Christlike love and nonresistance, bold evangelistic witness in word and deed, and a complete separation from the sin of the worldly social order. The church is the redeemed community, consisting of brothers and sisters living in holiness.

Menno Simons died January 31, 1561, in Wustenfelde, Denmark. Menno placed 1 Corinthians 3:11 on the title page of all his writings. "For no one can lay any foundation other than the one already laid, which is Jesus Christ."

Chapter 2
Birth of the "Brethren"

Migration to Poland

In the mid-1500s persecution and evangelistic impulses pushed the frontier of the Mennonite Church from Holland to the Vistula Delta of Poland near Danzig. Polish nobles welcomed the newcomers to their estates as farm laborers. The Mennonite immigrants drained swampy lowlands, built farms and, despite restrictions, established churches. For 250 years (1540-1790), Mennonites lived in religious and cultural isolation. They developed a lifestyle of religious tradition, cultural conservatism and lack of missionary vision that caused them to be known as "The Quiet in the Land."

The area came under Prussian rule in 1772. The pressure of Prussian militarism under Frederick the Great made it increasingly difficult for the non-resistant Mennonites. Mennonites' refusal to pay taxes to support the state church and the military establishment together with government restrictions on the purchase of more land for their growing families forced them to look for a new home.

Mennonite Colonies in Russia

Many Prussian Mennonites saw the land settlement policy announced in 1763 by Catherine the Great of Russia as providential. Russia was looking for industrious settlers for new territories acquired north of the Black Sea. Mennonites and other German immigrants were promised freedom of faith, nonparticipation in the military, land ownership and self-government. Starting in 1788, the Mennonites established German-speaking colonies of small villages with farmlands, church buildings, schools and homes. The early years on the Ukrainian steppes were difficult, but the industrious Mennonites eventually established themselves and by 1860 were a population of 30,000.

Ironically, by the mid 1800s the Russian Mennonite Church had taken on many of the characteristics of the European state church of the 1500s. Church membership was a prerequisite for civic privileges such as voting, land ownership and marriage. Baptism was extended to those who completed a catechism class, without insistence on personal commitment to Jesus Christ. Church elders began to act as civic authorities. Many elders showed no evidence of discipleship themselves. Church discipline, pastoral counseling and mutual care were often neglected. Divisions between wealthy members and the impoverished landless class deepened. Public drunkenness, gambling and moral decadence went undisciplined. The ordinances of the Lord's Supper and baptism took on a sacramental character, a sense that the rite itself replaced a need for disciplined Christian living. The Russian Mennonites faced social, economic, intellectual and spiritual stagnation. They were in need of renewal.

Revival Movements

The Mennonite colonies had not been without experiences of renewal, however. Between 1812 and 1819 small prayer circles began meeting in private homes. The groups became known for their study of the Bible and the writings of the early Anabaptists. These reformers sought a reawakening of early Anabaptist principles. Although threatened with exclusion by the ruling elders, this group was given recognition by the authorities as the *Kleine Gemeinde* (Little Church).

In 1822, a gifted teacher and spiritual leader, Tobias Voth, migrated from Prussia to the Ohrloff community. He organized prayer meetings and inspired students who later became leaders within the Mennonite Brethren renewal.

In the 1840s and 1850s, the center of the "Brotherhood" movement shifted to the village of Gnadenfeld, whose members had been influenced by Lutheran Pietists in Prussia and had migrated to the southern Ukraine in 1835 to escape pressure from the Prussian government. The Gnadenfeld Church promoted community and private Bible study and prayer, as well as the temperance movement. Most of the early Mennonite Brethren came out of this congregation.

The greatest catalyst for renewal among Russian Mennonites in the mid-nineteenth century was a Lutheran Pietist pastor, Eduard Wuest. After a personal conversion experience, he developed into a powerful preacher. Gifted with a commanding physique, melodious voice and attractive personality, Wuest was frequently a guest speaker in the Gnadenfeld Church. He preached a message of true repentance and God's free grace and called for personal commitment to "Jesus Christ, the Crucified." Many who were weary of lifeless formalism were drawn by his message into a vibrant spiritual relationship with God and each other.

A clash between Wuest's followers and the established Mennonite Church seemed inevitable, but Wuest himself died in 1859 at the age of 42 before the renewal could organize into a formal movement. Wuest had prompted renewal, but his own congregation allowed unbelievers to retain membership; he did not promote believers' baptism. Wuest was an important catalyst, but with his death the renewal movement turned to its Anabaptist roots for a New Testament concept of church.

Birth of the Mennonite Brethren

Many people had been converted to personal faith in Jesus in several villages of the Molotschna Mennonite colony in the Ukraine. The "brethren," as they called themselves, met regularly in homes for Bible study and prayer. These home Bible studies were the cradle for the birth of the Mennonite Brethren Church. Two developments brought about a break with the old church.

First, several small groups of the brethren (which also included women or sisters) requested a sympathetic elder of the Mennonite Church to serve them the Lord's Supper in their own home, according to Acts 2:46-47. They wanted to celebrate communion more frequently, but their request was also a reaction to taking communion with people who had made no open profession of faith. The elder refused their request on the basis that private communion was without historical precedent, would foster spiritual pride, and could cause disunity in the church. In November of 1859, the brethren decided to take the Lord's Supper in a home without the elders' sanction.

Second, church meetings were held to decide how to discipline the renegade revivalists. It appeared that reconciliation would be possible. Unfortunately, a few unsympathetic opponents attacked the leaders of the house Bible study movement, shouting, "Out with them; they are not better than the others [the ones who had participated in the private communion]." More shouts followed. About 10 men walked out of the church meeting. In all, the Gnadenfeld Church lost about 25 members to the house church movement.

On Epiphany, January 6, 1860, a group of brethren met in a home for a "brotherhood" meeting. This gathering proved to be the charter meeting of the Mennonite Brethren Church. They formulated a letter of secession that explained their differences with the mother church. The letter affirmed their agreement with the teaching of Menno Simons and addressed abuses they saw in baptism, the Lord's Supper, church discipline, pastoral leadership and lifestyle. Essentially, they were concerned that the church accepted members and leaders who gave no evidence of a redeemed and disciplined life as participants in the ordinances. Eighteen men signed the document. Within two weeks an additional nine men signed the letter of secession. Since each signature stood for a household, the charter membership of the Mennonite Brethren Church consisted of more than 50 people.

A similar, but independent spiritual awakening spontaneously emerged in the neighboring Chortitza Mennonite colony. It was characterized by conversions, Bible studies and renewal under Baptist influence. A visit of leaders from the Chortitza group to the brethren in Molotschna resulted in a baptismal service. These rebaptized leaders, subsequently, baptized others in Chortitza on March 11, 1862, the day recognized as the founding of the Einlage MB Church.

Reaction of the Mennonite Colony Administration
The Mennonite Church and colony hierarchy reacted swiftly

to the letter of secession. The church elders excommunicated the Mennonite Brethren and the colony administrative office prohibited further gatherings of the group, with violators subject to arrest and imprisonment. The colony also threatened exile, corporal punishment, social and economic ostracism, and the loss of civic privileges. Fortunately for the brethren, elder Johann Harder of the Ohrloff Church was more tolerant towards them, preventing administrative authorities from taking drastic action against the new group.

Johann Claassen acted on behalf of the newly organized brethren group to win official sanction from the Russian authorities and, subsequently, the colony administrators. Claassen made repeated trips to Petersburg to obtain government protection and to secure permission for resettlement for some of the group to the Kuban area in the Caucasus. Elder Johann Harder wrote a letter recognizing the Mennonite Brethren as a faithful Anabaptist Mennonite church. Although hostility between the groups was not eliminated by this act, the new group was on its way to recognition and acceptance by both colonial and national authorities.

A new church had been born. The desire for spiritual renewal, stricter church discipline and a fresh start had been realized. Unfortunately, the goals of the new movement were won at the cost of conflict and division. Historians have stated that some of the accusations against the "mother" church were too severe. Had the brethren been more patient, they would have seen that the revival that had begun in some of the congregations continued. Perhaps greater concern for unity would have allowed them to achieve their goals for renewal without a division.

Healthy emphases did, however, emerge with the birth of the new church. Mennonite Brethren taught the need for conversion based on the grace of God. Conversion involved repentance—a turning from sin to God. It was not simply a natural process involving learning the catechism. Baptism came to symbolize death to the old life and resurrection into the body of Christ and a lifestyle of discipleship. Communion, which included foot washing, was held more frequently. The church sensed the call to boldly proclaim the good news in evangelism, loving action and mission.

Migration From The Vistula To Southern Russia

Baltic Sea

Helsinki

St. Petersburg

Tallin

Novgorod

Riga

Dvina River

Moscow

Orsha

Dubrovno

Danzig

Koenigsberg

Mogilev

Thorn

Pripet Marshes

Dniepr

Gomel

Warsaw

Bug River

Pripyat River

Vistula River

Chernigov

Kiev

Poltava

Khar'kov

River

Dniestr River

Yuzhmy Bug River

Kremenchug

Ekaterinoslav

Prut River

Chortitza

Molotschna

Nikolayev

Kherson

Odessa

Berislav

Sea of Azov

Feodoslya

Sevastopol

Belgrade

Danube River

Bucharest

Black Sea

■ Mennonite Colony

•••• To Chortitza (1767-1789)

•—• To The Molotschna (1803-1804)

Map reprinted from the *Mennonite Historical Atlas*, page 13. Used by permission of Springfield Publishers.

Chapter 3
The MB Church Grows

Early Challenges (1860-65)
"The early history of the MB Church is not only characterized by controversy and conflict in its relations to church and state, but also by internal tension and turbulence among its members." So writes John A. Toews in *A History of the Mennonite Brethren Church*. The MB Church struggled in its early years to find a balanced approach to leadership and congregational organization.

One of the first issues to confront the new group was the mode of baptism. After a study of contemporary pamphlets on the subject, the Scriptures and the writings of Menno Simons, the church concluded that baptism by immersion was the correct biblical form. Eventually, participation in communion was limited to immersed members only, to the disappointment of a number of the early leaders. One hundred years passed before Mennonite Brethren reversed this stance and allowed membership to those who had been baptized upon confession of faith, regardless of the mode of baptism.

The emphasis on strong personal religious experience led to another controversy. Worship was characterized by informal spontaneity with the use of the vernacular Low German dialect. Traditional hymns introduced and closed the service, but the body of the worship time included lively contemporary songs, long audible prayers, and brief biblical exhortations interrupted by comments from the congregation.

The expression of personal spiritual experience became increasingly enthusiastic. Some leaders misinterpreted Eduard

Wuest's "joyous justification" doctrine and began expressing their new freedom and joy in an excessively emotional manner. This *Froehliche Richtung* (the joyous or exuberant movement) was characterized by intense enthusiasm (including noisy clapping and drum playing), false freedom (including brothers and sisters greeting each other with kissing, which led to moral sin), and spiritual dictatorship (including arbitrary use of the "ban" against those who disagreed with the excesses). The "June Reform" of 1865 reversed this excessive emotionalism. Excommunicated ministers were reinstated and wild manifestations in worship, including dancing, were condemned. The joy of the Lord was to be expressed in a "becoming" manner.

John A. Toews identifies six distinctive Mennonite Brethren emphases true to the early MB Church as well as today (pp.66-68). (1) The need for systematic Bible teaching is primary. Rejection of lifeless formalism leads to joyous expression, but this must be directed by thorough biblical instruction. (2) Because religious ferment is subject to powerful emotional expression with shallow intellectual consideration, there is a keen need for spiritual discernment. Emotion and personal experience are servants not masters; obedience borne of biblical study is to be our guide. (3) Leadership is to be entrusted to members with integrity and spiritual balance. (4) While strong and wise leaders are needed, dictatorship is suspect and to be rejected. Congregational participation and action are necessary for a strong church polity. (5) A strong ethical emphasis is needed. Happiness divorced from holiness leads to false freedom. Faith and practice must be kept in proper balance. (6) Meaningful church worship is essential. Lukewarm worship opens the door to hyper-emotional expressions. Radical renewal demands appropriate worship forms.

The First Migration to North America

The Mennonite Brethren Church in Russia grew rapidly. By 1872, twelve years after its founding, the Mennonite Brethren Church numbered about 600 members. Representatives met for the first MB Church family gathering, a time of inspirational meetings and planning for evangelistic church extension. A committee was elected to supervise the work of evangelism and five men were appointed to itinerant evangelistic ministry.

From 1874 to 1880, some 18,000 Mennonites migrated from Russia to North America, prompted by the Russian government's plans to introduce universal military service and economic factors. Among the immigrants were many Mennonite Brethren and a group of 35 families from the Krimmer (Crimea) Mennonite Brethren Church founded under Elder Jacob A. Wiebe in 1867.

The new settlers experienced all the hardships of pioneer life, including primitive sod houses, grasshopper plagues, lack of markets for their produce, and limited educational opportunities.

According to historian John A. Toews, church life in the early years (1874-79) in North America was also characterized by religious ferment and inner tensions. Settlers from different Russian colonies disagreed about issues such as mode of baptism and relations with Baptists and other groups of Mennonites. In 1878, the first interstate meeting of Mennonite Brethren leaders was held near Henderson, Nebraska, where the primary issue was uniting Mennonite Brethren congregations for mission purposes. An interest in evangelism and mission has continued to bind Mennonite Brethren congregations together through the years. Other early issues seem less significant today, including the "sister-kiss," head coverings for women, excommunication, mode of baptism and relations with Baptists (both union and communion were deemed unacceptable).

By the turn of the century, Mennonite Brethren congregations had been established in Kansas, Nebraska, North and South Dakota, Oklahoma, Colorado, Manitoba and Saskatchewan, and soon after in California, Montana, Texas, Oregon and Washington.

The Russian Revolution and Later Migrations

After 1875 the Mennonite Brethren who remained in Russia began to work in concert with the larger Mennonite Church. Joint conferences were held to discuss issues like baptism and the Lord's Supper. In 1884-85 large-scale revivals resulted in conversions, baptisms and growth in MB church membership. Strong MB leaders emerged, especially from the ranks of the teaching profession.

The three decades preceding World War I have been described as the "golden age" of the Russian Mennonite Brethren Church. MBs assumed positions of leadership within the larger Mennonite community. Mennonite colonies expanded into new settlements in many parts of Russia; these contained a high concentration of Mennonite Brethren. Educational growth, economic prosperity, forestry service as an alternative to military conscription, and the production and distribution of Christian literature characterized these years.

From its inception, the Russian Mennonite Brethren Church actively pursued evangelism and missions. Fulfilling the great commission was understood as fundamental to the church. Risk of imprisonment or exile did not keep people from witnessing to Russian neighbors. Evangelists distributed Bibles and witnessed to the good news. Because of a law prohibiting proselytizing, ethnic Russian converts were advised to join the Baptist Church. Participation in foreign missions began with financial support of mission societies and quickly moved beyond it, with the first MB mission field established in India.

Revolution, World Wars and Migrations

The prosperous golden age of the Russian Mennonite colonies was shattered by the events of World War I (1914-18) and the Russian Revolution (1917-18). Because their culture identified them with the German military foe, Mennonites experienced hostile treatment from the Russians. When German troops gained control of the Ukraine for a time, the Mennonites divided on the issue of nonresistance, with some forming armed units of self-defense. Later, it was recognized that this was not only a tactical blunder but a violation of their historic biblical nonresistance. The Mennonites of Russia were caught in the events of the Civil War that followed, as well as the terrors of bandit attacks. They experienced the ravages of malnutrition, disease epidemics and famine in 1920-1922. Relief assistance by European and American Mennonites, who organized to form the Mennonite Central Committee, finally arrived in March 1922, saving thousands from starvation.

During the time of war and anarchy, Russian Mennonites experienced widespread spiritual revival and engaged in unprecedented missionary outreach to their Russian neighbors. Communist policies allowed for open proselytizing among Orthodox Church members for a time. When the Communist government barred ministers from teaching in public schools, many Mennonite Brethren teachers were freed for evangelistic ministry. The revivals of 1924-25 not only fueled the fires of evangelism, but also enriched the Christian experience of many who fled Russia for Canada.

Some 18,000 Mennonites immigrated to Canada between 1923 and 1927, about a quarter of them Mennonite Brethren.

The Mennonites who were unable to escape faced the atheistic policies of the Stalinist regime. Church property was liquidated and religious freedom denied. Ministers were exiled to Siberian concentration camps or killed. Conscientious objectors to military service faced martyrdom.

From 1930 to 1940, anti-religious oppression was even more firmly institutionalized. German occupation of the Ukraine in World War II (1941-43) offered a brief interlude of relative religious freedom. When the German armies retreated, 35,000 Mennonites tried to escape with them. Some 12,000 eventually reached Western zones in Germany and migrated to Canada and South America.

PART TWO

Family
Distinctives

Chapter 4
People of the Book

Mennonite Brethren have always been known as "people of the Book." Study of the Bible sparked the renewal movement that birthed the MB Church. Envisioning those earliest days of MB life, various scenes come to mind.

First, one sees small groups of people in some of the Mennonite villages of southern Russia meeting in homes for Bible study and prayer. There is a lively give-and-take around the selected Scripture texts. Discussions are informed by reading materials provided by the Christian Literature Society organized by schoolmaster Tobias Voth. Issues that prompt further study include evangelism, world mission and a growing personal relationship with Christ. The writings of Menno Simons instruct the study. There is a decidedly intellectual stimulus, but the Bible study is not merely academic. It leads to repentance, conversion, revival.

Next, one sees two MB ministers meeting in the fields as they go about their farming. A controversial question is troubling the young church. How will they find direction? The two ministers lean against a fence post and reach into bulging coat pockets to retrieve their New Testaments. There is no WWJD (What Would Jesus Do) bracelet on their wrists, but both assume that the practical solution to a real problem will be found in this book. What Jesus teaches through his life and the Sermon on the Mount is the starting point for their search for direction.

Later, we see Bible conferences. Here dynamic preachers expound the Scriptures. High excitement is evidenced by standing-room only attendance. Tents are erected to contain overflow crowds. The Bible conferences are popular not only in the Russian colonies but in the Mennonite Brethren congregations of North America.

Finally, we see the church struggling for clear interpretation of biblical passages. Bibles are open and faces are taut with tension. Biblical study has not produced the expected consensus over the difficult question of freedom in worship. Elders have banned other leaders. Interpretation of Scripture promises unity even as it seems to provoke disintegration. Further study, further work together, is required. Eventually, it is community discernment in the Word, led by respected elders but including all members, that produces consensus, unity and satisfaction that the Spirit has illumined the church community's understanding.

These scenes from the past continue to be re-played in contemporary settings in the Mennonite Brethren Church. Commitment to studying and obeying the Word of God is at the core of who we are.

This chapter reflects on this important quality of our family life. What characterizes our understanding of the Bible? What do we have in common with other evangelical churches regarding biblical interpretation? What perspectives are distinctly Anabaptist and Mennonite Brethren?

Evangelical Pietist Influences

Mennonite Brethren share with Protestant reformers like Martin Luther the formula *sola scriptura, sola fide:* the Bible alone, faith alone. The early Anabaptists agreed that a hierarchical church authority, headed by the pope in Rome, had no right to decree Christian doctrine. Like Luther, early Anabaptist Bible students were expert in reading the Bible in their original languages and they agreed that the Bible should be translated into the common language of the people. Mennonite Brethren, while lacking the academic sophistication of Luther, shared the reformer's confidence in the Bible as the only guide for faith and life. They also accepted the Protestant canon of 66 books.

Several influences are evident in the Mennonite Brethren use of Scripture. The Mennonite Brethren have been particularly open to outside theological influences. Perhaps this is due to the circumstances of their birth. The relatively closed Mennonite society of mid-century Russia was opening to a larger world of technology, education, literature and religious ideas. This opening coupled with an intense desire for a deeper experience of God marked early MB experience. Among the movements that have affected MB interpretation are the sixteenth-century Anabaptists, nineteenth-century European Pietism, and mainstream evangelical-ism (including fundamentalism, Baptist theology and charismatic movements). More than most other Anabaptist-Mennonite groups, the Mennonite Brethren have been influenced by conservative Christian sources. This openness has both strengthened faithful discipleship, and threatened it.

Eduard Wuest, a Lutheran Pietist, contributed significantly to the religious awakening among Mennonites in Russia, and pietism continues to influence the Mennonite Brethren experience one-and-a-half centuries later. An explanation about the term "pietism" is in order. Piety, usually a word with positive connotations, describes holy living. Piousness, on the other hand, has negative overtones, and is associated with Pharisaic self-righteous hypocrisy. Pietism is a movement that emphasizes the personal religious experience. It carries the expectation that the Holy Spirit is present, active and powerful in producing spiritual growth.

In their book, *Only the Sword of the Spirit* (1997), Jacob Loewen and Wesley Prieb summarize the positive themes for which MBs are indebted to the Pietist movement. They include personal and small group Bible study; the call for a conscious and personal decision to accept salvation; a deeply-felt encounter with God; warm Christian fellowship; an emphasis on grace, Christ's return, personal evangelism and Christian unity; and a personal sense of God's call to congregational leadership.

Historically, the Baptist influence on MBs can be identified as a separate force. Theologically, however, the Baptists hold enough in common with the Pietists that their influence can be included under that broad stream. Like the Pietists, the Baptists were accepted because they shared the German language and culture with the Mennonites. Like the Pietists, they encouraged personal conversion, Bible study and evangelism. The Baptists were also important to Mennonite Brethren by influencing a congregational model of church governance, supplying an early confession of faith that was informally accepted for a time, and reinforcing the decision to institute immersion as the mode of baptism.

In North America today, the label given to Christians who stress orthodox theology is "evangelical." Mennonite Brethren share with evangelicals a concern for personal evangelism, conservative biblical interpretation, personal piety and salvation by grace. We promote evangelical cooperation by joining national evangelical and mission organizations. We cooperate in broader evangelistic outreach and parachurch agencies.

The historical emphasis on experiential faith and the ongoing work of the Holy Spirit has also opened Mennonite Brethren to continuing charismatic influences. Many MBs have adopted much of the music and theology of these movements. Charismatic sign gifts, post-conversion experiences of the Holy Spirit, and spiritual warfare have attracted interest. Mennonite Brethren continue to converse with one another about the compatibility of these influences with our distinct theological perspective.

Not all aspects of pietism and evangelicalism have positively influenced the MB Church. Loewen and Prieb, for example, identify the following concerns. Emphasis on a personal conversion experience at a specific date intensifies the emotions involved and confuses the fact that coming to faith usually involves a process. Emphasis on personal spirituality suggests a private faith and erodes Anabaptist understandings of the New Testament, which places obedience and discipleship within the church community. Historically, Baptist connections created various ethical and doctrinal tensions between MBs and other Mennonites. Finally, the militaristic orientation of the German Baptists and some of the Pietists is alien to the Mennonite understanding of Jesus' teaching.

The Anabaptist Interpretation of Scripture

Mennonite Brethren recognize and appreciate that pietism and conservative evangelicalism have shaped their interpretation of the Bible. But Mennonite Brethren also hold that their approach to Scripture is distinctive because they retain an Anabaptist "hermeneutic" or method of interpretation. This is seen particularly in their approach to the Bible and in interpreting Scripture as a faith community.

The early Anabaptists practiced a "focused canon" in contrast to a "flat canon" (Loewen and Priebe).

The flat canon argues that, since the Bible is the Word of God, every word must be given equal weight. This approach thus concludes that the Old Testament primarily addresses nation states and sanctions, for example, the use of military force. The New Testament, by the same approach, is seen as addressed primarily to individuals and reinforces the pietistic emphasis on individual encounter with God. The flat canon fails to give primary weight to the life and teachings of Jesus, which is seen by Anabaptists as the canon's center. It also distorts and avoids the Old Testament emphasis on covenant relations, justice and concern for the stranger.

Mennonite Brethren follow the focused canon approach. This does not relegate parts of the Bible to secondary status but instead reveals the unity of the biblical message. Christ is at the heart of this message. Nothing in the canon is ignored in the interpretive process, but the meaning of all parts is understood through the life of Jesus.

MBs also accept the Anabaptist notion of what is called "community hermeneutics or interpretation." This means that our interpretation of Scripture depends on the process of reading and discerning the Bible together as a Christian family.

Community hermeneutics was important in the early days of the Anabaptist reformation and in the birth of the MB Church. It was the issue that caused the Anabaptists to split with the reformer Ulrich Zwingli in the Swiss reformation of the early sixteenth-century. Zwingli allowed civil authorities to limit the church's practice of, and understanding of, the New Testament. The Anabaptists insisted that the community of faith should read the Bible together, then put its understanding of the Bible into practice.

Similarly, the 1850s renewal in the Russian Mennonite communities was born of Bible study in small groups. The early Mennonite Brethren settled controversial questions by deliberating together as a community of faith and limiting the authority of individuals, even if they were leaders. They developed the practice of Bible study conferences, in which biblical texts were explained and studied together.

MB Principles of Interpretation

The MB Confession of Faith recognizes three specific principles of biblical interpretation. First, the entire Bible is Spirit-inspired. Second, the Holy Spirit guides the community of faith to interpret the Spirit-inspired text. Third, Jesus is the lens through which all Scripture is to be interpreted.

Let us consider these three principles by referring to the *MB Confession of Faith*.

1. "We believe that the entire Bible was inspired by God through the Holy Spirit...We accept the Bible as the infallible Word of God and the authoritative guide for faith and practice" (Matt. 5:17-20; 2 Tim. 3:14-17). When we confess that the Bible is inspired, we are speaking about the authority of Scripture. The Bible is our guide because it is God's Word to us.

Mennonite Brethren accept traditional, orthodox categories to describe the revelation of God. We recognize that God speaks through creation, God's judgments and grace, and human conscience; this is called general revelation. But only through God's special revelation do we learn that God initiated a covenant relationship with Israel through Abraham, Moses, David, Jeremiah and others. Through special revelation, God communicated the very being of God in the person of Jesus Christ. The written Word, the Bible, is the means by which God's special revelation is made available to us.

MBs have struggled to find the proper terminology to describe their high view of Scripture. In the fundamentalist-evangelical debate of the 1970s, some argued for use of the phrase "inerrancy of the Bible." For most of those favoring this term, inerrancy described the original documents (the text as penned by the biblical author) and understood the Bible to include truth about science, geography and history as well as theological truth. Others argued in favor of a different terminology. They pointed out that the original documents are no longer

PEOPLE OF THE BOOK

available to us. They noted that the Bible does not claim authority in matters such as science and geography. In fact, biblical authors seemed to adopt the conventions of their day in speaking about the universe.

Mennonite Brethren have settled on the language used in our Confession to make two emphases. First, the Bible is "the infallible Word of God. " This term supports the understanding that the Bible cannot mislead us regarding God's will. It is a completely reliable source for revealing God's Word to us. Second, the Bible is "the authoritative guide for faith and practice." Our emphasis is not simply on right doctrine (orthodoxy) but on faithful obedience (orthopraxis) as well. The Bible has the authority to call Christians to follow the way of Jesus. The authority of Christ's life and teaching is passed to the church as a call to church discipline (Matt. 18:15-20). The Bible guides the faithful practice of the redeemed community.

2.   We believe that "the Spirit guides the community of faith in the interpretation of Scripture." As stated earlier, community hermeneutic is a central and distinctive element in our understanding of Scripture.

In practical terms, community hermeneutics of Mennonite Brethren means that Christians are encouraged to study the Bible in personal reading and in small groups. Teachers who have learned to discern God's will by living in the community of believers and who have interpretive tools—perhaps knowledge of the original biblical languages and understanding of the various literary styles in the library that makes up the Bible—assist in the process. Their authority is no greater than other participants because of their academic preparation, however; they serve the community with their assistance.

When an issue becomes too complex or divisive to resolve in a local congregation, we consult our brothers and sisters. We try to follow the model of Acts 15, where delegates gathered in Jerusalem to discuss the entrance requirements into the church. MBs have traditionally depended on a group of leaders (called by various names in the past such as General Conference Board of Faith and Life, or Board of Reference and Counsel) to identify

31

issues in need of broader discussion. The board members usually study the issue, then call for a study conference where the Bible is studied in small groups and through written papers and messages. The board then tries to discern a consensus, which they present as a resolution at a convention of delegates from all churches, where it undergoes furthers discussion, leading to a decision.

Community hermeneutics operates with several assumptions. First, we assume that the Holy Spirit is active within believers to illumine the Scriptures. We do not expect new revelation or a new authoritative word from God, but we do expect illumination and fresh insights. Second, we believe it is the role of the community to test illumination against Scripture. Is it consistent with Jesus' teaching, the New Testament, the Bible as a whole? Third, we can expect differences of opinion. Community hermeneutics is tested in times of conflict. While conflict may be healthy (1 Cor. 11: 19), communication in these situations must be characterized by charity and mutual trust. Fourth, community hermeneutics calls for faithful practice, not simply true doctrine. The test of a biblical people is their lifestyle.

3. We believe that "God reveals Himself supremely in Jesus Christ, as recorded in the New Testament." Here our Confession reminds that we hold to a Christ-centered interpretive strategy, one of the distinctives of Anabaptist theology. Jesus' person, life and teaching reveal God, and thus Jesus is the lens through which all Scripture is to be interpreted, and the authority by which it is to be obeyed.

   This interpretive principle has sometimes been called "progressive revelation." Some scholars use this term to mean that religion generally, and Israelite religion specifically, began with crude ideas about God that were refined through an evolutionary process. This is not the view of Mennonite Brethren.

   Rather, we see the Bible as the story of God's work in the world. As the story progresses, so does our understanding of God's purpose. From the beginning, God works as Creator and Redeemer. As God's work unfolds, we are better able to interpret God's purposes. In the person of Christ, we gain significant new insight into God's will. This new Word, Jesus Christ, enables us to make better sense of parts that were formerly unclear.

We understand that the place to begin biblical interpretation is Jesus' Sermon on the Mount (Matt. 5 to 7) and its parallel texts. We take these texts as Jesus' challenge to the church today, not as an idealistic program for some future kingdom of heaven.

Jesus develops three themes in his proclamation of the kingdom of God in which we participate. First, he blesses the poor. Jesus' message is that God's rule is good news for the poor (Luke 4:18-19). He speaks frequently about freedom from attachment to things. He calls for radical generosity. Generosity-to-the-point-of-poverty is one of the themes of Anabaptist Christ-centered interpretation.

Second, Jesus calls his followers to peacemaking. When we confess our sins, we have peace with God. That inner peace motivates us to pursue peaceful relationships with those around us, beginning with our families, our communities, and even extending to our enemies. We see this as a vital part of Christian discipleship.

Third, Jesus calls for community. Jesus teaches that the only way to practice his impossible ethic is together with our brothers and sisters. Being salt and light in the world is not a call to radical rugged individualism. It is an invitation to a covenant community, which we call the church family.

The Mennonite Brethren interpretive strategy reminds us that the end of Bible study is not simply knowledge or understanding but faithful obedience to the example of Jesus. We meet Jesus in the text and discover he asks for extravagant generosity. He models life-giving peacemaking. He invites us to be part of a family that teaches and practices this kingdom lifestyle.

Chapter 5
The New Testament Church

Life as a Family

My teenage son is intrigued by his family tree. While he has traced his ancestry to the eighteenth century, his interest is a limited one. He is more curious about ancestors than second cousins. Other family members will need to pick up that angle of our family lines.

As MBs we too like to trace our family back to its roots. We see the original, first-century church as the model for our life together as believers. We study the book of Acts and Paul's letters for clues about family relations. The Gospels also direct us to what Jesus, our eldest brother, had to tell us about family life.

Interest in our New Testament origins sparks a second interest. How are we related to our closest church family members? In this chapter we want to reflect on the New Testament church model and some of the family traditions that tie us together as MBs. Just as some biological families stand out because they share the trait of red hair or unusual musical talents, so we as MBs are known for family values that are distinct, perhaps even unique.

Growing the Family

The New Testament teaches that good family life is essential for a healthy relationship with the Father. Just as babies are nurtured best when they are born into a family, so evangelism and conversion are a family affair spiritually. Our confession (Article 7, "Mission of the Church,") points to twin truths regarding evangelism. First, evangelism is the responsibility of every believer.

"The Holy Spirit empowers every Christian to witness to God's salvation." Second, evangelism is a function of our life as a family. "The church as a body witnesses to God's reign in the world. By its life as a redeemed and separated community the church reveals God's saving purposes to the world."

The New Testament church was an evangelistic church. The book of Acts repeatedly records astonishing numbers of people who repent, believe, are baptized, and join the family of God. Pentecost, "the birthday of the church," was an event of corporate witness (Acts 2:2,14).

The sixteenth-century Anabaptist church, as we saw earlier, was keenly evangelistic. The nineteenth-century Russian Mennonite awakening which produced the MB Church was evangelistic in character. The contemporary MB Church continues to make evangelism a focus. Healthy MB congregations continue to plan local outreach through friendship evangelism, special events, children and youth programs, and ministries to people in need in their circles of influence. As a larger family, MBs plant churches in North America and around the world.

Redemptive Discipline

In the New Testament church family, discipline nurtured healthy relationships between spiritual siblings and with God. Our Confession of Faith (Article 6) describes the MB interpretation of church discipline: its purpose is to win the erring sibling back into fellowship (Matt. 18:15-20).

The early Anabaptists described active church discipline as one act that distinguished them from the state church. The nineteenth-century revivalists also were active in the practice of discipline. They chided the "mother church" for failing to discipline pastors and other members for drunkenness and other public expressions of unfaithfulness. MBs limited the celebration of the Lord's Supper to those who were willing to live within a covenant of faithfulness.

Since the 1860s, the MB Church has struggled to find balance in the practice of church discipline. Church records show that conference proceedings often dealt with questions of ethical practice. In the early years, the conference prohibited things such as carrying life insurance, joking and jesting among members, attending circuses and theaters, viewing television and permitting women to worship without proper head covering. Many issues of earlier times appear legalistic to contemporary observers, but they demonstrate the seriousness with which MBs have taken the call to holiness.

The MB Church continues to hold expectations about behavior that fits a follower of Christ. Our Confession of Faith (Article 12) forbids the swearing of oaths (Matt. 5:33-38; cf. James 5:12). Other prohibitions include social sins such as drunkenness, smoking and gambling. While these rules may seem to border on legalism, they also serve as a reminder that the believer is not to conform to the world.

The late Mennonite scholar John Howard Yoder once declared that following Jesus meant imitating Christ in one, and only one, dimension: radical social nonconformity. Today, MBs struggle with knowing how to be witnesses to the gospel of peace in the midst of a society that values institutional violence, affluence and self-gratification. Rejection of abortion and sexual license are values MBs share with other evangelical Christians. We continue to struggle toward consensus on issues such as capital punishment, carrying handguns, divorce and remarriage, and accumulation of wealth.

Baptism and the Lord's Supper

Every family has rites and passages that define membership. The Mennonite Brethren Church celebrates two rites—baptism and the Lord's Supper, which we call "ordinances" or "signs." Using the term "sign" distinguishes MBs from those who attach God's mediating grace to these acts and call them "sacraments." MBs are also distinguished from those who call them "symbols," as only symbolizing an internal reality. The notion of "sign" is a biblical term, pointing to God's saving acts (Exod. 10:1; Acts 4:16) and to human action (Exod. 12:13). Baptism is a sign of commitment, and the Lord's Supper a sign of covenant loyalty.

BAPTISM

From the beginning of the New Testament church, one act publicly identified those who had been adopted into the family of God.

Believers were baptized upon confession of faith and were "added to the number" of those who composed the local congregation. Baptism is the rite of passage into the covenant community.

The Great Commission (Matt. 28:19-20) has a single command: "make disciples of all nations." Two explanatory phrases define disciple making: "baptizing them" and "teaching them to obey my commands." Why is baptism so important?

First, baptism is "a sign of incorporation into the body of Christ as expressed in the local church" (Confession of Faith). Biblically, baptism is described as "into Christ" (Rom. 6:3; Gal. 3:27; 1 Cor. 10:2) and "into one body" (1 Cor. 12:13). The phrase "into Christ" describes incorporation into the community of which Jesus is the head. Old distinctions of class, race and gender are erased. Baptism unites very different people, even former enemies, into one body.

On Pentecost, those who accepted the evangelistic message "were baptized and...added to their number." Acts 2:42-47 describes church life following Pentecost: "...the Lord added to their number daily those who were being saved" (v. 47). Both references link baptism to inclusion in the church. One cannot belong to Christ without belonging to the church. One cannot belong to an invisible, universal church without a simultaneous commitment to a local, visible congregation.

Second, baptism means cleansing. In the words of the Confession, "Baptism is a sign of having been cleansed from sin. ...that a person has repented of sins, received forgiveness of sins, died with Christ to sin..." Immoral behavior is inappropriate for those who have been washed and sanctified through baptism (1 Cor. 6:11). Christ has cleansed the church to make her pure, holy and without blemish (Eph. 5:26). The cleansing power of the cross, which is significant in baptism, makes the former way of life off-limits.

Third, baptism symbolizes the new life of salvation. "We believe that when people receive God's gift of salvation, they are baptized...[They have been] raised to newness of life..." Baptism is associated with new life, life in the kingdom of God and fullness of life in Christ (Col. 2:12). We are buried with Christ in his death and raised with him to newness of life.

Baptism is offensive to modern sensibilities in several ways. First, it is an ancient rite. Baptism was a common first-century marker for conversion to Christianity, Judaism and other religions, and may seem like a holdover today.

Second, baptism marks a clear break from the past. In regions where Christians are persecuted, it is baptism that defines the change of commitment. Muslims, Hindus, Buddhists and Mormons in varying ways could accept a "Jesus-in-my-heart" prayer while ostracizing, perhaps even persecuting, a person who is baptized to join the community of Christ's followers.

Third, baptism provokes controversy because it demands commitment to the family of Jesus. In North American communities that lack clear teaching about baptism, it is the commitment to a specific church family that sparks controversy. Some prefer to say "Yes" to Jesus and his universal, invisible body but to say "No" to the body of Christ in a specific community. Just as the resurrection body of Christ had real "physicality," so the body of believers is always a community of real "flesh-and-blood" people.

Historically, for Anabaptists this biblical understanding was very costly. Following the Roman Catholic lead, mainline Reformation churches baptized infants to wash away original sin and to bring them within the covenant community. Anabaptists agreed that baptism was the rite of incorporation into the covenant community. But they disagreed that the faith of the parents or the church was sufficient for the event to have meaning. Instead, the Anabaptists taught that each member needed to make a public confession of faith in Jesus to be saved and to join the community of the redeemed. As we have seen in chapter 1, this view of baptism led to bloody persecution.

The nineteenth-century Mennonite Brethren reformers insisted on a return to believer's baptism. Even though the Mennonite Church in the colonies did not baptize infants, citizenship was restricted to baptized church members. Catechisms were recited from memory and personal commitment to Christ was neglected.

The birth of the MB Church forced the community to develop its own baptismal practices. How would the new church practice believer's baptism? The issue of eligibility was of first and foremost concern. They concluded that baptism is for "those who confess

Jesus Christ as Lord and Savior and commit themselves to follow Christ,...for those who understand its meaning, are able to be accountable to Christ and the church, and voluntarily request it..." (Article 8).

Candidates for baptism must take the initiative in requesting baptism. The one requesting baptism is given instruction regarding its meaning and the ensuing commitment to the local church. Newly baptized believers commit themselves to the practice of mutual accountability for disciplined obedience. Baptism is seen as a commitment to the Lordship of Christ.

MB congregations have struggled, at times, with the appropriate age for baptism. There is no hard-and-fast rule, but the wording of our Confession is meant to encourage young believers to wait for baptism until they can function as accountable church members. Generally, early adolescence has been seen as the age of accountability. By the time they reach adolescence, most prospective baptismal candidates can understand the concepts inherent in baptism and can legitimately confess that they will renounce friendship with the world in return for membership in God's family.

Another question for the emerging MB Church was that of baptismal mode. MBs settled on immersion. The Krimmer Mennonite Brethren branch had the distinction of baptizing forwards (usually in running water). Today MB churches are free to immerse in water that best suits the purpose of the event. Some congregations use baptisteries; others find lakes or rivers; some employ tanks, tubs or swimming pools. Most congregations follow baptism with formal reception of the newly baptized members into the church and with the celebration of the Lord's Supper.

THE LORD'S SUPPER

The Lord's Supper is the second ordinance or sign practiced by the Mennonite Brethren Church. Like baptism, the Lord's Supper is understood to be a covenant event. If baptism is the sign of entry into the covenant community, the Lord's Supper is the sign of unity with the body of Christ.

Like baptism, the meaning of the Lord's Supper played a significant role in the origins of Anabaptism and, later, of the MB Church. The Swiss Anabaptists and Menno Simons agreed that the bread and the cup were signs of Christ's body and blood.

They rejected the Roman Catholic belief that the bread and the cup were changed into Christ's body and blood (transubstantiation) and the Lutheran doctrine that the elements contained the spiritual presence of Christ (consubstantiation). In Russia in 1860, the celebration of the Lord's Supper outside a church building was seen as an act of defiance that eventually led to separation from the Mennonite Church and the founding of the Mennonite Brethren. The MBs held that the Lord's Supper was an event reserved for faithful disciples and should not be celebrated with those who rejected a godly lifestyle. Further, they requested communion in their homes in order to celebrate more frequently, more intimately, and in a context of greater faithfulness.

A series of biblical themes informs Mennonite Brethren understanding of the Lord's Supper. First, the bread and the cup point to Jesus' sacrificial death on the cross. Among MBs, two theories about Jesus' atoning death are informative. One, the judicial interpretation, sees the atonement as the payment of the death penalty by the innocent victim. The other, the *Christus victor* model, views the atonement as Christ's defeat of the enemy at the cross.

Second, the phrase "the cup of the new covenant" centers on the covenant theme (Matt. 26:26-29; Mark 14:22-25; Luke 22:14-22; 1 Cor. 11:23-26). As Christ's physical body is one, so the covenant community forms a single body. Fellowship, the product of intimate relationships with Christ and with one another, marks the people of God. The Lord's Supper symbolizes unity.

Third, the Supper anticipates the future, that is, the fulfillment of the reign of God at the messianic banquet celebrated with His redeemed church. In 1 Corinthians 11, Paul reminds the church that "you proclaim the Lord's death until he comes" with the Supper. The Supper looks forward to the great marriage supper of the Lamb at the end of the age.

The question of **who** should be allowed to participate in the Communion has often been controversial. Are only baptized believers eligible? Only those baptized as Mennonite Brethren? Do MBs hold to "closed" or "open" communion?

In the 1980s and 1990s, many MB congregations began offering communion to anyone who confessed Jesus as Savior. The new openness reflected an interest to include believers who had not yet formalized their membership, believers who had been baptized as infants but were unwilling to be rebaptized and children too young for baptism. Recognizing the practice of the church the Confession of Faith speaks of extending participation in the Lord's Supper to "all those who understand its meaning, confess Jesus Christ as Lord in word and life, are accountable to their congregation and are living in right relationship with God and others." Our Confession also acknowledges that the normal New Testament pattern was that baptism preceded participation in the Lord's Supper.

Application of this biblical principal calls for parents and church leaders to work together to ensure faithful participation in this covenant act. The invitation to participation must always be coupled with a call to self-examination. The church is responsible to practice discipline, repentance, confession and renewal when there is a breach in relationships within the congregation.

The MB Church has no established directive regarding frequency of communion. Practice generally varies from quarterly to monthly commemoration. MBs have shied away from weekly participation lest the event become superficial and hurried. Restricted, private communion celebrations (including its use at weddings to symbolize the marriage union) are inconsistent with our theological understanding.

The New Testament practice of breaking bread together daily and weekly in homes was a powerful witness to their intimate fellowship. The need to balance the New Testament emphasis on the Supper as a church event and the first century pattern of house churches suggests further reflection together how the church can best remember the Lord's death, recognize the Lord's body, and anticipate the Lord's return.

One other covenant event—foot washing—has, historically, been associated with MB church life. Although it is no longer regularly practiced in most MB congregations, the rite is increasingly popular among younger members as an expression of unity. Foot washing can be a worship event reminding family members "of the humility, loving service, and personal cleansing that is to characterize the relationship of members within the church" (Article 6).

Living as a Family

Every family develops routines and traditions. These include weekly household chores, Christmas preparations and family vacations. We have been looking at the traditions associated with the special family events, but now we turn to our understanding of how the church is nurtured from day-to-day and week-to-week. For the MB family, growth as disciples of Jesus is our primary aim.

Mennonite Brethren hold that discipleship is nurtured within the church community. The primary purpose of church life, we believe, is to nurture our members to live as faithful followers of Jesus. Worship, fellowship, Bible study and outreach all contribute to the growth of the community of disciples.

God equips us for service by empowering us with the gifts of the Holy Spirit. MBs believe that the spiritual gifts listed in the New Testament continue to be operative today. We also believe that, since no New Testament list is complete, the Spirit may empower the use of other abilities, such as music or drama, as spiritual gifts. The key to using all the gifts, especially the so-called charismatic or sign gifts (speaking in tongues and prophecy), is that they build up the family as a whole. While some MBs encourage the development of tongues as a personal prayer language, more emphasis is usually placed on other gifts.

Congregational Polity

Mennonite Brethren do not have a prescribed congregational structure. Local bodies choose their own form of leadership structure. An elder board or a church council governs most MB churches. The congregation is also given a voice in major decisions. Increasingly, larger congregations look to the pastoral staff for initiative in planning.

At its birth, the MB Church reacted against what it perceived to be arbitrary and unspiritual pastoral leadership in the mother church. Insisting on the priesthood of all believers, the church was cautious about giving pastors too much authority. MBs recognized the need for wise, strong leadership balanced by congregational participation. They also quickly recognized the need to unite in larger inter-congregational groups, called conferences.

Congregations set their own direction for local ministry but they work together in these regional and national conferences to do church planting, world mission, higher education, larger youth events, pastoral leadership development, nurture and credentialing. Currently, the values of localism and individualism are challenging that healthy tradition. Commitment to the larger family groupings will demand continued vigilance by church leaders and fellowshipping congregations.

Chapter 6
Peacemaking

The *Martyrs Mirror* tells the stories of 800 Anabaptists who died because of their commitment to the good news. One of these, Dirk Willems was imprisoned for his faith, condemned to death, emasculated by a diet of bread and water, yet escaped from his second story cell. Pursued by a prison guard, Willems raced across a frozen pond to freedom. The pursuer, well fed and well clothed, fell through the thin ice. He cried out for help. Since Willems alone heard the cry, he felt constrained by the love of Christ to rescue his foe. Willems was subsequently rewarded for his merciful act by being recaptured and burned at the stake (Bragt, 741-42).

A more recent story of meeting violent threats with the good news of Jesus took place in Kinshasa, Congo. Pakisa Tshmika met Bertrand in church one morning in 1997. Bertrand had recently escaped from his homeland, the Central African Republic, where he had been unjustly imprisoned for contesting election fraud. The military government in Congo plotted to kidnap Bertrand and return him to his country for execution. When Pakisa became aware of the plot, he and his family decided to provide Bertrand safe haven in their home, knowing that if found, they would also be incriminated. One day the presidential secret service showed up at Pakisa's house, threatening violence. Pakisa invited the agent, armed with a machine gun, into his house for tea. Pakisa shared the message of Jesus' love with the agent but refused to release Bertrand. Pakisa asked the agent to inform the people who sent him that they would have to kill him first before they could have Bertrand. Agents came to the house every day for weeks to threaten Pakisa and his family. Pakisa responded with loving hospitality. Finally, God opened the door for Bertrand to escape to a friendly West African country.

Willems and Pakiska illustrate what MBs believe about peacemaking. Peacemaking is active, evangelistic and Jesus-centered. It is rejection of violent retaliation. Peacemaking begins when we find peace with God. Peacemaking is a realistic alternative for those who live within the supportive context of the faith community.

Jesus calls us to join the peacemaker family. He opens his State of the Kingdom address (the Sermon on the Mount) with the Beatitudes (Matt. 5:3-12). In the Beatitudes, Jesus blesses peacemakers. By calling peacemakers "children of God," Jesus is announcing that peacemakers are particularly like God. He then offers a series of case studies to illustrate how he came to fulfill the law through a "greater righteousness." The six contrasting statements show how Jesus transforms a legalistic interpretation of the Law into the active righteousness of peacemaking (Matt. 5:17-48).

Jesus' words against violent retaliation have been the foundation of Anabaptist commitment to peacemaking. Although his strategy has been commonly labeled "pacifism" or "nonresistance," Jesus *does* call for resistance. But, as Walter Wink points out in his article, "The Third Way," it is the nonviolent resistance of evil. Jesus' words are best interpreted, "Do not react to violence with violence" or "Do not use evil in your fight against evil."

Understanding the cultural context of Jesus' sermon gives fresh insight to Jesus' examples. When Jesus teaches us to turn the other cheek, he is commending a nonviolent strategy of resistance that avoids either extreme of the fight/flight option. To strike on the right cheek involves an insulting backhand administered by a superior to an inferior. Violent reaction would be suicidal. No reaction would be cowardly. Jesus commends neither. Instead, Jesus calls the insulted, lower rank person to "turn the other cheek." This has the effect of forcing the aggressor to treat the victim of violence as an equal. In this example, and in those that follow, Jesus calls for the use of humor and creativity as well as strength to absorb the violence, to defeat violent evil.

Active peacemaking is underscored in the sixth contrasting statement (Matt. 5:43-48). Jesus overturns the conventional principle which says, "love your neighbors but hate your enemies" by challenging us to love even our enemies. Jesus is describing an evangelistic strategy. Pray for your persecutors, Jesus says, reminding us that the Beatitudes are tied closely to the contrasting statements that follow. Peacemaking seeks to fulfill Christ's mission for the church, to fulfill our Lord's command to make disciples of all nations (Matt. 28:18-20). Followers of Christ seek to turn enemies into friends. This lifestyle is risky, demanding, sacrificial, but it is the way of Christ.

The only way that the call to radical peacemaking can become a practical part of the Christian life is for the family of God to covenant to be active peacemakers together. The apostles recognized that peacemaking was the fundamental guiding principle for forming the family of God. Jesus came to restore the broken relationship between God and humanity. Jesus created a new family out of formerly warring factions (Gal. 3:26-28). He tore down the barriers that divide people and created a new family in which enemies have been reconciled to live as brothers and sisters in Christ (Eph. 2:11-22).

The New Testament letters describe members of the believing community as ministers of reconciliation. They serve their enemies (Rom. 12:20; 13:8-10), return good for evil (Rom. 12:17, 21; 1 Pet. 3:9), pursue peace with all people (Rom. 12:18; 1 Pet. 3:11) and follow the example of the one who refused to retaliate (1 Pet. 2:21-25). It is only by living within the community of peace that its members are empowered by the Lord and Spirit of the community to fulfill their ministry of reconciliation (2 Cor. 5:11-21).

Third Millennium Peacemakers

The MB Confession of Faith emphasizes the positive and active quality of peacemaking. We confess that "[b]elievers seek to be agents of reconciliation in all relationships. ...Alleviating suffering, reducing strife, and promoting justice are ways of demonstrating Christ's love." Our Confession calls us to obey Jesus' command to do good to those who hate us (Luke 6:27-28).

MBs have understood that these teachings are to be applied in a number of ways.

Peacemaking begins at home. The church is to take the lead in bringing peace to homes and families, to be an advocate on behalf of victims of spousal and child abuse, to foster reconciliation by teaching families to resolve conflict without violence.

MBs oppose violence against vulnerable members of the human race. We oppose violence against unborn children. One cannot be pro-peace without also being pro-life. In Article 14 we confess that "[t]he unborn, disabled, poor, aging and dying are particularly vulnerable to...injustices. Christ calls [us] to care for the defenseless."

MBs are not immune to church conflict. The church is called to be a community of peace where the healthy exchange of differences brings reconciliation. MB churches have at times established covenants to guide their communication. These covenants encourage the practice of honest, loving exchanges and renounce gossip.

MB churches are faithful to Christ by showing leadership in helping to resolve neighborhood disputes, racial tensions, and animosity between victims of crimes and their offenders. Many MBs work in mediation services which aim to bring people together for restitution and reconciliation. We encourage prison visitation programs as well as rehabilitation and re-entry of prisoners into society.

Active peacemaking is also the aim of several inter-Mennonite agencies in which MBs participate. Mennonite Central Committee (MCC) provides relief to wartorn areas. MCC Peace Section addresses international concerns. Mennonite Disaster Service (MDS) works at peacemaking by serving communities that have faced natural disasters. The story of these agencies is told in chapter 12.

Peacemaking begins in restoring our relationship with God, then with our intimate family and friends and moves into ever-widening circles, through acquaintances, our workplaces and to the world at large. This leads us to consider how MBs respond to war.

The early Anabaptists taught that "the use of the sword" was contrary to the teachings of Christ. They opposed the use of force by the state to enforce particular Christian beliefs.

The Anabaptists recognized that nations had a legitimate duty to use the sword for police action. Menno Simons witnessed the tragedy of the Peasant Revolt in which early radical reformers were crushed after seeking to defend an independent state; that event helped convince him to lead the Dutch Anabaptists in the way of Christ.

MBs in Russia also struggled with the issue of "the sword." In the terror-filled chaos following the 1917 revolution, Russian Mennonites organized a self-defense force. Later, after suffering heavy losses, they repented of their violent strategy. Historian John A. Toews calls the action "not only a tactical blunder, but also a gross violation of historic biblical nonresistance. It must always be regarded as a dark blot on the pages of Mennonite history" (Toews, 108-9).

Today the MB Confession of Faith addresses the issue of military involvement as follows: "In times of national conscription or war, we believe we are called to give alternative service where possible." MBs are grateful to God that governing authorities in North America have provided alternative service for those who choose not to enter military service. The MB Church is called to counsel youth to offer themselves in loving service to reduce strife and alleviate suffering rather than to take up arms in military conflict (Commentary/Pastoral Application, 150-51).

MBs have come to this conviction about the implications of Jesus' call to love the enemy because we see peacemaking as a way of life. Nonresistance is not an awkward accessory that needs to be pulled out in times of war. The power to return love for hate comes from our new nature in Christ. The Spirit enables us to live faithfully by providing a supportive community of believers within the family of God.

Peacemaking includes a call to prayer. Followers of Jesus pray for their enemies (Matt. 5:44), and for government officials and those in authority (1 Tim. 2:2). They pray for bold proclamation of the good news of peace (Col. 4:4). Prayer is part of the believer's spiritual armor, enabling us to take our stand in the great conflict with the principalities and powers of this evil world (Eph. 6:10-18).

What about members of our congregations who disagree with this position? What about MBs who serve in police forces where lethal force is sometimes expected in the line of duty? These questions and others are raised in the pastoral commentary on Article 13 of the Confession of Faith. The response there upholds the notion that this Article is so central to our identity as Mennonite Brethren that our leaders must agree to teach the way of peace. We accept members who do not endorse some details of Article 13 if they are willing to join with an attitude of submissiveness and teachability.

Challenges to Active Peacemaking

Two objections might be raised to peacemaking as God's way for God's family. First, doesn't the Old Testament teach that God endorses the use of violence by nation-states? Second, can anyone point to modern examples of this type of radical peacemaking, even on a small scale?

OBJECTION #1: OLD TESTAMENT WAR AND PEACE

For some, God's commands to destroy Israel's enemies seems an ironclad objection to the Anabaptist interpretation of Jesus' words. If God orders war in the Old Testament, isn't Jesus simply referring to personal relations? God surely has not changed His mind about war, has He?

First, as MBs we begin with Jesus, not the Old Testament. We understand that Jesus speaks the clearest word from God and we interpret the rest of Scripture in light of what he said and did. Jesus clearly calls us to love our enemies. There is no hint that the ethic of Jesus changes for citizens of warring nations. For Jesus, our primary citizenship is in the kingdom of heaven.

Second, we as Anabaptists note that in the Bible, life and death are in God's hands. God's first act with the nation of Israel was the miraculous deliverance from Egypt through the Red Sea. According to Exodus 12-15, Israel was called to witness God's deliverance and judgment. Egypt, the aggressor and oppressor, received the judgment due their rebellion against God.

Third, the Old Testament includes a tradition in which God's ways are the way of peace. The psalms speak of God's act of delivering Israel and destroying the weapons of war (Pss. 37:14-15; 46:9). The prophets look forward to a day when war will cease and Israel will fulfill its role of being a light to the nations (Isa. 2:4; 60:1-3).

Fourth, when the Old Testament attributes the commands to go to war to God, the battle plans are unconventional by any modern standard. Trumpets and faith count more than weapons (Josh. 6; 10; Judg. 6-7; 2 Chron. 20). Weapons gained as spoils of war are destroyed as part of God's policy (Josh. 11:9; 2 Sam. 8:4). It is hard to justify modern warfare by turning to the Old Testament. This review suggests some of the ways MBs have responded to the objection that the Old Testament seems to approve war. It is noteworthy that the just war theory, a primary Christian alternative to nonresistance, is based on New Testament peace teachings rather than reference to Old Testament war stories. This just war theory seeks to limit violence by protecting noncombatants. Just war theory is a strategy of last resort, deemed necessary as the lesser of two evils in a fallen world. The MB strategy of peacemaking calls for Christians to reject all forms of war. Instead we seek to trust God to provide a means to restrain evil and to protect the innocent.

OBJECTION #2: CAN CHRISTIANS LIVE IN THE WAY OF PEACE?
Some may object: Isn't the Mennonite interpretation of Jesus' words impractical? Does the way of peace work?

MBs have always been grateful for freedoms offered in nations in which they have lived as pilgrims and strangers (1 Pet. 2:11). True nonresistance, however, depends on God, not guns, for protection. In the spirit of the three Hebrew youths who refused to worship the image of the empire in Daniel 3, we confess that "our God is able to save us, but even if he does not, we will not worship the image." Faithfulness is a higher value than freedom. Obedience to God ranks higher than human life itself.

So, our ethics are not determined by how well they work. We do not practice peacemaking because it makes us successful. On the other hand, reports abound of how peacemaking produces good results. Allow one story from the Revolutionary War to suffice.

Michael Whitman, a British loyalist from Pennsylvania, spat in the face of Mennonite church leader Peter Miller. Miller refused to retaliate. A few days later, Miller received word that Whitman had been sentenced to be hung for treason by General Washington.

Miller walked to Valley Forge to beg for Whitman's life. Washington asked Miller what Whitman had done for him that would impel him to walk 70 miles to save his friend's life. "Friend? He counts himself my bitterest enemy," replied Miller. "In that case," replied Washington, "I issue a pardon on the condition that Whitman is charged to your care." Miller and Whitman returned home, no longer as enemies but as friends.

Church and State

Closely related to the question of peacemaking is the issue of the Christian's relationship to the state. As noted above, MBs have been grateful to God for governments that have allowed them freedom of conscience. At the same time, in Article 12 of the Confession of Faith, we confess that our primary citizenship and allegiance belong to Christ's kingdom, not the state or society.

We see the government as part of God's plan to give order to society. God has instituted government structures ("principalities and powers" of Eph. 6:12, Rom. 13:1-5) to reward good and restrict evil. To the extent that government promotes well-being and maintains law and order, it is acting according to its God-given mandate. When governmental demands contradict God's will, our responsibility as Christians is to "obey God rather than humans" (Acts 5:29).

Traditionally, Mennonites have held a separationist attitude toward government. This attitude grows out of the notion, expressed in the Schleitheim Confession of 1527, of two orders, "one inside the perfection of Christ and the other outside the perfection of Christ." According to this view, government exists for the world. The state uses coercion and violence to keep evil in check. Christians cannot be involved in such actions. Increasingly, however, MBs have become active in local, provincial, state and national governments.

Article 12 of our Confession reminds us that as Christians we are to "cooperate with others in society to defend the weak, care for the poor, and promote justice, righteousness, and truth...and to witness against corruption, discrimination, and injustice...." We have already addressed the call to be conscientious objectors to military service. What other issues demand a faithful witness?

God calls us to have a broader vision for our corporate witness. In an increasingly diverse society, we are challenged to witness against racism, sexism and classism. We are called to share power within the denominational structures with other ethnic groups whose membership is growing among MBs. We are challenged to respond compassionately to immigrant brothers and sisters, keeping in mind that as spiritual "aliens" in this world we are to show hospitality to strangers (Deut. 24:17-18; Matt. 25:31-46; Heb. 13:1-2). We are challenged to recognize and resist the idolatrous temptation to put our own economic security ahead of those experiencing overwhelming poverty in other parts of the world.

We believe the Bible teaches that there is a close relationship between social relationships and the issue of integrity and the oath. Mennonites have enjoyed a reputation as people who speak the truth. Mennonites take literally the prohibition against swearing of oaths (Matt. 5:33-37; James 5:12). Refusing to take an oath is a witness to our commitment to speak the truth at all times, whether under oath or not.

Chapter 7
Disciples Are Missionaries

Clint grew up in a North American household where "Jesus" was used only as a swear word. When Clint reached adolescence, he got mixed up with the street drug culture. Clint did everything he could to fit into the drug scene. He wore ragged leather clothes, grew long, ratty hair, and tattooed his arms with suggestive images. Under evil influences, Clint would experience paranormal behavior and speak with voices he did not recognize. When his mother became a Christian, she started praying for Clint, asking Jesus to free him from the influences of Satan. According to Clint, one day something seemed to click. Instead of resisting Jesus, he asked Jesus to deliver him from sin. The change was miraculous. Clint went from selling drugs to telling his former drug customers about Jesus. Sometimes they got angry. Sometimes they listened to the good news of Jesus. Today Clint is involved in an MB church in a large city and is considering how to use his evangelistic gifts in urban church planting. Although Clint is happy to tell what Jesus has done for him, he also tries to make it clear that the testimony of a person who grew up in a Christian home is just as strong a witness for God's saving power. Clint has experienced what MBs believe: to follow Jesus one not only receives salvation from God but shares God's love with others. Members of the family invite others to become part of God's household of faith.

Jesus' command, "Go and make disciples of all nations" (Matt. 28:19-20) is the starting point for MB thinking on salvation. Jesus inaugurated the reign of God, saying, "The kingdom of heaven is near. Repent and believe the good news!" (Mark 1:15).

Then he directed the call to specific individuals. "Come," he said, "follow me" (Mark 1:17).

Mennonite Brethren believe that the call to follow Jesus begins with a call to personal conversion. The context for conversion is "the kingdom" or "reign" of God. In his parables, Jesus interprets the kingdom as the community of those who do God's will. The will of God is counter cultural, a radical departure from the established order.

Jesus' first word of command is "Repent." Repentance involves a new way of thinking, new action. For Israel, Jesus' announcement of the rule of God meant God was calling out a new people irrespective of nationality or ethnicity. For us, it means getting our minds around the idea that our purpose has changed. We turn from being centered on self to serving others.

The word "turn" points to the action-side of the repentance theme. MBs have used the word "conversion" to describe the turning from sin and turning to God. The earliest revival of Eduard Wuest in Russia, which paved the way for the MB founding, emphasized the importance of conversion. Conversion was an invitation to a sure and personal experience of salvation in Jesus Christ, as opposed to simply a "memorized faith," as had become the church tradition among Russian Mennonites.

Conversion freed the seeker from guilt, granted peace with God, and promised the assurance of salvation. The emphasis on a specific experience of conversion had great integrity when applied to adults who understood the theological principles of the gospel but needed to appropriate it to their own lives. A psychological struggle with guilt and the breakthrough to a new commitment fit their context. Conversion was an event in the larger experience of salvation. Those who converted to Christ gave evidence of a changed life, were baptized by immersion, and were accepted into the membership of the congregation.

Most testimonies of those raised in MB homes tell of children who "accept Jesus into their heart" in a crisis moment in the home, at church programs, or in summer camp. Others accept Christ later in life. Some come to a moment of conviction and are gloriously transformed. For others, coming to faith is more of a process than a single event. These adults often witness the faithful life of a

Christian acquaintance, explore the life of the faith community, hear repeated explanations of the gospel, and find themselves confessing their own allegiance to Christ without being aware of a crisis of conversion. The emphasis on an experience of the revivalist model is not as strong today.

MBs continue to insist on a personal, living faith as a mark of conversion. We use biblical language to say that we are "born again" as we join the family of faith. We are adopted as God's children.

Let's review. "Conversion" is the word used to describe the experience or process by which a person becomes a follower of Christ. "Repentance" is the act of turning from sin to God which goes along with a new mindset that accepts God's rule. "Salvation" is what God does in giving grace to a sinner. Salvation describes conversion, repentance, faith, baptism and joining the church. Salvation is what God has done at conversion, what God continues to do in transforming us to be like Christ, and what God will finish when we are received into God's presence as part of the new creation. Salvation includes the growth in Christ that comes as the Holy Spirit indwells the believer, producing the fruit of the new life.

Mennonite Brethren emphasize that God's saving act joins us to the community of faith. We grow in discipleship as we experience the accountability of the body. Our aim is to grow to be like Christ. We grow both as we are nurtured and as we serve others. (See chapter 5 for a more complete description of the way we encourage family members to grow as disciples.)

World Mission

From the start, MBs have perceived faithful disciples to be both "salt" and "light." Faithful discipleship ("salt") expresses itself in a life of witness ("light"), locally and globally. In the Great Commission Jesus calls us to make disciples of all nations. According to the late MB church leader J. B. Toews, the Mennonite Brethren Church is a renewal missionary movement. Since the 1890s, MBs have sent missionaries around the world.

In *A Pilgrimage of Faith*, Toews describes the beginnings of MB missions. One early leader was Peter Wedel, an effective itinerant evangelist in North America. At the 1884 General Conference in South Dakota, Wedel shared with the delegates his growing burden for unreached people in other lands. The conference pleaded with Wedel to continue his evangelistic ministry rather than go to the Cameroons, a country known as a westerner's graveyard because of its treacherous climate and raging black fever. Wedel spent the night walking the cornfields and seeking an answer from God. Wet with the morning dew, he announced to the convention, "Obedience supersedes all other opportunities. I cannot but go to the Cameroons." Within a year of his departure, Wedel was dead, a victim of black fever. His death sparked a dramatic movement. Others followed, going not only to Africa, but to India and China as well. Wedel's act of obedience became a cornerstone of MB foreign missions (Toews, 97).

Historically, the impetus to organize in a denominational or institutional sense can be attributed, in large part, to the desire to do mission in a way characterized by MB distinctives. These distinctives reflect the evangelical Anabaptist roots of Mennonite Brethren. First, MB mission is inspired by an evangelistic motivation—to proclaim in word and deed, the good news of Jesus Christ. Second, the effort is church based, both in its sending and in its goal. The covenant community discerns, calls out, sends, supports and receives missionaries. The purpose is to plant Bible believing churches. Third, mission is kingdom centered on holistic ministry to the poor. When the Board of General Welfare (charged with assisting MB refugees from Russia) combined with the Board of Missions, organization was following theology. In our largest mission efforts, the most receptive response has come from the poorest segment of society.

At first, it was easier for MBs to evangelize in other cultures than among closer neighbors. Mennonites migrated to Russia with an explicit agreement not to proselytize Russian Orthodox Church members. MBs sent their first missionaries to India, but also began to evangelize closer neighbors. In the first half of the twentieth century in North America, Mennonite Brethren did evangelistic work among German and Russian speaking neighbors but apart from a mission to the Comanche Indians and several city mission projects, did little witnessing among English-speaking neighbors.

They were much more aggressive in sending missionaries to other countries, principally Congo, India and China.

Since World War II, MBs have been much more active in domestic church planting. During and after the war, congregations moved away from using the German language to avoid identification with the Nazi regime. They engaged in North American life through their alternate service activities which helped them become aware of social needs, especially in public mental health. The alternate service communities became the nucleus for urban and suburban churches. Today, both national conferences and most district and provincial conferences have active programs for launching new churches. Chapters 9 and 10 outline our progress in domestic church growth.

The international mission program of North American MBs began in 1898. Peter Wedel had been accompanied by his wife Martha and Henry and Maria Enns in the mission work with the Baptists in the Cameroons. In 1899 the first conference-appointed missionaries, N.N. and Susie Hiebert, left to serve among the Telegu-speaking people of India. Although forced to return because of ill health, Hiebert became a leader of MB mission efforts.

Early international mission has been characterized as having a "family spirit" (Clarence Hiebert, *Christian Leader,* December 2000, 5). Missionaries were known personally to the sending churches. Congregations were well informed about missionary activities and organized church life to promote missions. Sunday school teachers and parents prayed that their children would be called into ministry. Women formed missionary societies to pray, correspond with missionaries, gather supplies for the poor, and raise funds. The church called out its most gifted leaders, including Tabor College presidents H.W. Lohrenz and A.E. Janzen, to administer the mission efforts. Missionaries served extended terms of service, sacrificing family, wealth, health and even life itself.

As a result, churches were established. India and Congo, the earliest "fields" with the largest missionary staffs, now number over 92,000 and 84,000 members respectively. After World War II, mission outreach proliferated, with new fields opening in Paraguay and Colombia, then Brazil, Peru, Japan, Mexico, Ethiopia, Germany, Austria and Panama. By the 1950s, North

American missionaries totaled 279. Efforts were made toward indigenization and urban ministries.

The middle decades of the twentieth century brought turmoil to missions. Revolutions swept out colonial governments. Under the direction of J.B. Toews, indigenization characterized MB mission policy. As the MB mission handbook states, "With the growing international rejection of all colonial imperialism, there has also arisen a principal rejection of the 'missionary-centered gospel ministry.'"

Under this emerging attitude, North Americans no longer saw themselves as caring for infants and children, but sharing with sisters and brothers. The family relationship matured to the current policy of partnership. The name of the denominational mission agency changed. Out was the old central planning agency of Board of Missions and Services (BOMAS). In was Mennonite Brethren Missions and Services International (MBMSI). Today national churches determine direction and invite North American partnership as needed.

In 2001, MBMSI had mission involvement in 65 countries with 49 traditional career missionaries (now called "multi-term core missionaries"), 65 multi-term core-plus workers (missionaries working in such categories as joint appointment with Wycliffe, tentmakers who have income-generating work, missionaries sent by a national MB conference like Japan, or teachers sent to a receiving agency as Pan American Christian Academy in São Paulo), and 5 single term core missionaries (including English teachers in China and Japan). MBMSI "partners" with national churches in the support of 450 national evangelists and church planters. National churches are organized in 19 countries worldwide. Their story is introduced in chapter 11.

MBMSI involvement in Botswana illustrates the cooperative ventures that characterize contemporary MB missions. MBMSI has worked as a partner in the Africa Inter-Mennonite Mission (AIMM) since the 1970s. In 1992 Byron and Teresa Born began a Bible teaching ministry there. They work with African Independent Churches (AIC). AICs address such African felt needs as disease, witchcraft and ancestral worship. Born reports that some AICs are quite orthodox in their commitment to God's Word and Christ's saving death and resurrection while others remain rooted in African traditional taboos. These churches encourage culturally relevant worship forms, including drums, hand-clapping and dancing. The Borns teach biblical foundations and discipleship as they encourage theological reflection. Their ministry has expanded beyond Bible teaching to pastoral care as the HIV/AIDS epidemic has invaded the church (based on articles in the July 2001 MBMSI *Witness* magazine authored by Jeanine Yoder).

At the start of the new millennium the watchword for international missions is the "10/40 window." At the time of writing, four billion people live between the 10th latitude south and the 40th latitude north and 90% of them have never heard the Christian message. MBMSI is at work in 26 of these countries of which 15 have MBMSI core missionaries.

The newest venture is Team 2000. Six people and their young families have made a 10-year commitment to church planting among unreached people in an urban center of Thailand.

Several issues stand at the forefront of MB mission at the beginning of the twenty-first century. First, "globalization" has brought mission to our own doorstep. MBMSI contributes to the support of Ethiopian, Slavic, Kosovar, Korean and Khmer congregations in North America. Japan has sent missionaries to plant a church in California and another to Thailand. MBMSI regional directors in Europe, Africa and Latin America hail from the areas that they direct. MBMSI is planning on incorporating board members from other national conferences beyond Canada and the U.S.

Second, "localization" threatens binational partnership. The General Conference structure which previously owned MBMSI has been dissolved. Local congregations find priorities which compete with denominational missions. Some congregations have turned their focus from the world to their own neighborhood. MBMSI is seeking ways to encourage local evangelistic initiative while continuing to help the larger North American family cooperate to reach the world.

Third, "participation" has an entirely new meaning. In a world that has shrunk to the milliseconds it takes to communicate with someone around the globe, secondhand mission reports lose luster next to firsthand mission experience. In 2000, short-term mission travelers outnumbered long-term missionaries by about 20-to-1. Short-term ministry offers opportunities for a closer look at the international church, exposure to international church planters, and the direct challenge to give more generously or to consider personal long-term ministry.

But there are also dangers in reliance on short-term missions. Usually, evangelizing with integrity requires time to build relationships, familiarity with culture, and facility with communication. A quick, up-close study may actually provide less perspective than a thoughtful report from far away. Stewardship is also an issue. Are funds diverted from effective, economical long-term projects for exciting but expensive short-term trips? Or, more positively, do mission trips to difficult Third World situations replace luxury vacations to tropical resorts? Short-term mission endeavors require thoughtful vigilance to ensure that they contribute to long-term church health, just as the sometimes paternalistic approaches of the past did.

The MB family is a worldwide clan now. We share a common vision. Jesus calls people in all parts of the globe to be converted, to become members of the discipling community, and to proclaim Jesus' good news for the poor.

The Ways Missionaries Are Sent

	Multi-Term Missionaries Core	Multi-Term Missionaries CorePlus (MAs)	Single-Term Missionaries Core	Single Term Missionaries CorePlus (MAs)	Global Volunteers (includes YMI and CPE)	Partner Workers (approximate)
1996-97	62	30	2	3	325	728
1997-98	56	38	1	2	313	730
1998-99	49	44	5	2	439	450
1999-2000	55	56	5	5	907	450
2001	49	65	5	21	910	450

Chapter 8
Working Together

Daniel grew up in a rather typical rural MB congregation on the prairies. He accepted Jesus as his Savior at vacation Bible school in the summer after grade 5. His faith was nurtured by Sunday school teachers who regularly attended Christian education workshops sponsored by the MB conference. At home his parents read the *Christian Leader* which encouraged them in their nurture of their children. Every summer in junior high and high school Daniel attended an MB church camp where he accepted the challenge to follow Jesus as the Lord of his life. His MBY was active, and Daniel traveled with them to the national youth convention while he was in Grade 11. There Daniel not only got to know other MB youth from across the continent but was challenged by the dynamic speakers and worship to commit his life to Christian service.

After Daniel graduated from high school, he began attending Tabor College, a few hours from his home, in pursuit of a business degree. His spiritual commitment waned, and after his first year he left Tabor to attend a state university. While there, Daniel joined the party scene and drifted from his commitment to Christ and the church. Then Daniel was invited to a parachurch ministry retreat where he came under conviction for his wayward path. The next year Daniel returned to Tabor, earned a double major in Bible and computer science, and became active in campus ministries. He participated in a mission trip to the Anabaptist Mennonite Mexico City church, a trip jointly sponsored by the college and Youth Mission International. After Dan graduated from Tabor, he got a job with a computer business in his hometown. He married his college sweetheart, helped with the youth group, and preached occasionally.

Daniel continued to feel the call of God on his life. He sensed the need for seminary training and sought counsel from his pastor and his former college professors. Although his boss at work offered him a full scholarship to another denominational seminary, Dan headed to Fresno, California to attend MBBS. Dan is active in Butler Ave. MB Church and plans to return to the Midwest to pastor after he graduates from seminary.

Daniel's story is like that of many who have been nurtured in the MB Church family. Godly families seek to be faithful to the biblical admonition to "train up a child in the way he should go" (Prov. 22:6) and to teach the love of God to your children "when you are at home and when you are away, when you lie down and when you rise" (Deut. 6:7). As the MB family has grown, we have sought to nurture faithfulness to our identity as God's family through education, media and youth ministries.

The MB family was born in Bible study and nurtured through Christian literature and Christian education. As we have grown, MBs have organized to foster discipleship. We have developed institutions of higher education, Christian education, youth ministry and camping, literature and other media, and resource management.

J. B. Toews (*Pilgrimage of Faith,* 168) points out that the North American MB Church has faced the conflicting demands of communal cohesiveness and of a shared relationship with prevailing culture. It soon became evident that cultural isolation demanded in the Russian setting, and pursued in the rural communities of North America, would not be maintained. Toews concludes:

> The Mennonite Brethren Church, with a world-wide constituency in an age of religious pluralism, cannot continue to sustain itself with an implicit, experiential theology. The challenge for MBs...is to renew the process of a community hermeneutic to interpret their faith and life in the context of modernity....conference leadership will need to accept major responsibility for this vital process. (186)

This chapter describes some of the institutions that the MB conferences in North American have founded to help fulfill this responsibility.

Higher Education

U.S. LIBERAL ARTS COLLEGES

Soon after their arrival in the American Midwest, MBs sensed the need to provide college education for church leadership. For seven years several leaders of the fledgling conference operated the German department at McPherson (Kan.) College as a first step toward establishing their own college. In 1908, with local MB leadership, Tabor College and Academy in Hillsboro, Kansas, began to offer Christian liberal arts education. The MB General Conference heard regular reports from Tabor and offered periodic financial support. In 1933, after learning that Tabor had produced more than 100 missionaries, pastors and evangelists but faced foreclosure due to the Depression, MBs officially adopted Tabor as the conference school. From 1944 to 1955, the Bible Department served as the MB school of theology, offering the Bachelor of Divinity program.

Tabor College has been served by many MB conference leaders and trained many more church workers. The late historian John A. Toews wrote that Tabor's "spiritual impact on the educational and missionary endeavors of the MB conference can hardly be overestimated" in its role as "the chief training ground for church leadership" (*MB History,* 273).

Today Tabor College is an accredited four-year Christian liberal arts college governed by the Southern, Central, Latin American and North Carolina MB district conferences, offering 35 majors in the Bachelors of Arts program, a degree completion program, and two masters degrees.

Regional and national needs led to changes in Tabor College's role as the sole provider of higher education for the denomination. In 1944, two schools that eventually evolved into universities began offering classes: Pacific Bible Institute in Fresno, California and Mennonite Brethren Bible College (MBBC) in Winnipeg, Manitoba. In 1954, the higher education program of the MBs was nationalized with the newly formed U.S. conference taking responsibility for Tabor, Pacific and the emerging MB seminary and the Canadian conference maintaining governance of MBBC.

Fresno Pacific has grown from a Bible institute to a fully accredited Christian university offering liberal arts-based undergraduate, graduate and professional studies. "The Fresno Pacific Idea" grew out of the school's roots in Anabaptist and evangelical ideals. Now owned and governed by the Pacific District Conference, FPU has been recognized for its quality as a regional private liberal arts college. It offers bachelor degrees in 41 fields of study as well as graduate degrees in education, business, and conflict management and peacemaking.

CANADIAN BIBLE COLLEGES

The Canadian Conference established Mennonite Brethren Bible College to prepare students for church-related ministries. To that end administrators developed a faculty of well-known conference teachers, leaders and ministers. Within its first two decades the school produced some 500 ministers, teachers and missionaries. Changing needs proved the catalyst for transforming the mission of the school. In 1992 the college was renamed Concord College, reflecting a new focus on liberal arts training. Governance was shifted from the Canadian Conference to the provincial conferences of Ontario, Saskatchewan, Alberta and Manitoba. In 1999 Concord joined the new Mennonite Federation to form Canadian Mennonite University. CMU offers a Bachelor of Arts degree as well as bachelors degrees in church music, musical arts and church ministries. The School of Discipleship, supported by the Manitoba MB Churches, offers an eight-month program in Bible study, work projects, faith formation and cross cultural experience.

Columbia Bible College grew out of Bible classes conducted in Abbotsford, British Columbia in the late 1930s. In 1943, three churches combined to give official status to the school. The school's growth has been marked by its adoption by the British Columbia MB Conference in 1960, merger with a school sponsored by the Conference of Mennonites in 1970, accreditation as a Bible college in 1982, and a charter to grant theological degrees by the provincial legislature in 1987. With a Bible-based Anabaptist educational program designed to prepare students for discipleship, service and ministry, Columbia offers a Bachelor of Arts (with majors in biblical studies, caregiving and counseling, early childhood education, church ministries, mission, outdoor recreation leadership and youth), as well as one- and two-year certificate, diploma and adventure-based discipleship programs.

BIBLE SCHOOLS AND CHRISTIAN HIGH SCHOOLS

The Bible school movement has been called a unique MB contribution to Christian education, especially in the Canadian prairie provinces. The Bible institutes drew young people into Bible study, especially during winter months when farm work was minimal. These schools served to instruct young people regarding peace and nonresistance, provided theological fundamentals, preserved a Christian worldview, and prepared youth for service in the church. Until the late 1960s, some 17 Bible schools flourished under MB auspicious. In 2001 only Bethany Bible Institute remained and retained its Bible school status, though they too were in the process of changing their status to a Bible College. As noted above, Pacific Bible Institute has become a university and Columbia Bible Institute is now a Bible college.

Bethany Bible Institute was founded in Hepburn, Saskatchewan, in 1927, after winter Bible classes had been held in nearby congregations for a decade or more. Bethany benefited from the spiritual leadership of well-known MB teachers and leaders. The school is sponsored by the Alberta and Saskatchewan MB Conferences and, since 1995, the Saskatchewan Conference of the Evangelical Mennonite Missionary Churches. Bethany identifies itself as a Christian training center founded in the evangelical Mennonite-Anabaptist tradition and includes in its mission objectives equipping men and women in discipleship, biblical studies and practical ministries in church leadership. Bethany offers two-year diploma and certificate biblical studies programs, three-year bachelors of Christian ministries and four-year Bachelors of Arts degrees.

MB high schools, related to the Bible school movement provide an education that seeks to integrate faith and learning at the secondary school level. These schools include Corn (Okla.) Bible Academy (since 1902); Immanuel High School (Reedley, Calif., 1912); Mennonite Educational Institute (Abbotsford, BC, 1944); Mennonite Brethren Collegiate Institute (Winnipeg, Man., 1945); and Eden High School (St. Catharines, Ont., 1945).

ECOLE DE THEOLOGIE EVANGELIQUE DE MONTREAL

In the province of Quebec, the Ecole de Theologie Evangelique de Montreal (ETEM: the School of Evangelical Theology of Montreal) provides training for ministry and Christian life. It was originally established as the Institut biblique Laval (IBL) in 1976. ETEM currently is in association with the University of Montreal and the Institut Biblique Europeen in Paris, France. It is one of only two accredited university-level evangelical schools in Quebec. ETEM has played a key role in equipping not only Quebeckers, but immigrants whose first language is French. In Quebec the evangelicals number about half of 1% and Mennonites are viewed by some people as a cult. This ministry provides visibility, credibility and stability to the Mennonite-evangelical community.

An important feature of ETEM is the Centre for Research and Development. It is focused on providing French language curriculum for children's Sunday schools—the only one of its kind in North America. It sells materials in francophone countries all over the world, to evangelical, mainline Protestant and Roman Catholic churches.

BIBLICAL SEMINARY

The shift from multiple lay ministry to professional pastors in the 1930s and 40s in the U.S. and within the next decade in Canada precipitated a concern for denominational pastoral training. As an interim measure, the Tabor College Bible department offered a seminary program from 1944 to 1955. In 1955 the U.S. conference founded Mennonite Brethren Biblical Seminary in Fresno, California. Pacific Bible Institute and Tabor College provided senior faculty members as teachers and administrators. In the 1960s, during the presidency of J.B. Toews, the Seminary established itself as an Anabaptist learning center, emphasizing biblical theology and practical congregational ministry. In 1975 the Canadian conference joined the U.S. to sponsor a unified seminary program. Until 1995 the Fresno campus served MBs from Canada, U.S. and around the world. At that time, the need for an increase in the number of trained pastors, coupled with the desire of many potential seminary students to study closer to home, led to the establishment of the MBBS-BC Centre in Abbotsford, British Columbia. The dissolution of the General Conference in 1999 further complicated governance issues. MBBS has continued to provide a unified theological education program with study centers in Fresno, Abbotsford, and most recently in Winnipeg. MBBS-BC is part of the ACTS (Associated Canadian Theological Schools) Consortium located at Trinity Western University in Langley, British Columbia. Henry Schmidt, who began teaching at the Seminary in 1972 and was appointed seminary president in 1992, guided the Seminary through these rapidly changing approaches to education.

The Seminary offers a Master of Divinity degree and several Master of Arts degrees, which allow the students to choose an emphasis that meets individual needs. Pastoral leadership, preaching, Bible, pastoral care and counseling, missions, and church planting are among the possible emphases. In addition, the Seminary offers a degree in Marriage, Family and Child Counseling, which meets California requirements for licensure as a therapist. The Seminary has shaped a generation of MB leadership by preparing pastors, missionaries, counselors and church leaders. From an evangelical-Anabaptist orientation, it aims to inspire and equip men and women to live as disciples of Jesus Christ, and to serve and lead in the church and world. The Seminary includes students from many denominations but remains rooted in the Anabaptist and Evangelical traditions.

DIRECTION

Cooperation among Mennonite Brethren educational institutions is reflected in *Direction* journal, published semiannually in hard copy and, since early 2001, also on its own web site. Beginning in 1972 as a partnership among four educational institutions, *Direction* is now subsidized by all six MB postsecondary schools in North America. The journal's mission is to provide a forum for conference leaders, pastors, educators and informed church members in which to address biblical, theological, historical, ethical, pastoral, educational and evangelistic concerns, from international as well as from local perspectives. Seeking a role complementary to the denominational periodicals, *Direction* often fosters the practice of community hermeneutics by featuring articles that deal with ethics, contemporary faith issues, Christian education, science and faith, worship, evangelism and mission, social concern, pastoral care, and Mennonite Brethren history. Issues that deal with such current concerns as spiritual warfare allow the scattered denomination to "meet" through print and, more recently, through its web site.

Youth Ministries and Camping

In local congregations Mennonite Brethren train youth and children through Sunday school, vacation Bible school, midweek programs and youth ministries.

Denominational ministries have emerged to encourage local efforts in evangelizing and discipling youth. In 1971, the first Canadian national youth convention, called "Banff 71," attracted about 700 youth and adults. The convention has been held every three years since then, moving away from The Banff Centre in 2002 in order to accommodate larger numbers of registrants. In the U.S. the first national youth convention was held in Glorietta, New Mexico in 1975. Since that time, U.S. MB youth have met every four years, usually in Estes Park, Colorado. These major programs for challenging youth to deeper Christian commitment have resulted in new prayer movements, evangelism and commitment to build youth groups at home.

Camping has been an important means of nurturing spiritual growth. In Canada eight camps and conference centers owned by MB conferences or societies in six provinces provide ministry to thousands of children, youth and families every year. In the U.S. Southern District camping is organized as a ministry of the Youth Commission. Other districts also encourage growth through conferences and camps but without formal denominational leadership. Many young people mention youth camps and conferences as the settings in which they accepted Jesus Christ as Savior and renewed faith commitments.

Youth Mission International (YMI) began as a centennial project of the Canadian Conference. In 1988, at the Winkler MB Church, located in Manitoba, a group of 100 young adults was dedicated for practical and evangelistic ministry that summer. Since then, young people in both Canada and the U.S. participate in YMI programs which have grown to include a high school summer service and a year round training program. Many countries of the world have been touched by young Christians who have undergone spiritual renewal and training in an intense week of preparation. The impact has been felt in addition to local church ministries and by overseas mission workers. In 2000, YMI joined MBMSI, the missions/service ministry to unify our system for developing young missionaries and church leaders.

Christian Education

The Canadian Christian Education Board was established in 1963, to oversee Sunday school and midweek ministries for children and youth. The board held some very successful CE worker training events, drawing 600-700 people from across the country. In addition, the board developed music programs and liaisons with camping ministries.

One key role for the board has been evaluating and writing curriculum. Early on the *Adult Quarterly* (now evolved to *Word Wise* and published by Kindred Productions for both the Canadian and U.S. churches) was created to help adults study the Bible. Mennonite Brethren from both Canada and the U.S. cooperated with other Anabaptist denominations to create Sunday school curriculum in the 1970s (The Foundation Series) and in the 1990s (*Jubilee: God's Good News*). Midweek club programs, adult Bible studies and parenting video series represent some of the material that have been assessed.

As times change, strategies adjust as well. Greater emphasis on mutual equipping has led to youth and children's ministry worker networks. *Ideabank*, the newsletter for CE workers is available both in print and on the web site.

In the U.S., Christian education has also been encouraged through denominational structures. After the U.S. reorganized, primary leadership was shifted to district Christian education committees which have developed resource libraries and training resources.

Denominational Christian Education administrators assist with evaluating and writing curriculum.

Publishing

Distribution of Christian literature in the Russian colonies was one catalyst for the renewal that produced the MB Church. MBs continue to be active in communicating the good news through various media, especially publication.

Mennonite Brethren churches in Canada and the U.S. are currently served by five periodicals published in four languages. *The Christian Leader* is the publication of the U.S. Conference. It is an English-language publication made available to all United States MBs. The Canadian Conference supports four publications. The *Mennonite Brethren Herald* is the English-language publication, *Le Lien* is a French-language magazine, the *Mennonitische Rundshau* is a German-language publication with a broad international readership and the *Chinese Herald* serves the growing number of Chinese churches. These publications give writers within our denomination the opportunity to exercise their gifts and keep the denominational family informed of events at the national and local level. The magazines also provide a place for instruction, inspiration and dialogue on issues relevant to the readers.

Kindred Productions, the publication arm for the Canadian and U.S. Conferences, has been active in producing inspirational books, a New Testament commentary series and curricular materials. The inspirational books are designed to tell stories that point everyday people to an everyday God. The Luminaire Study series is designed to assist in Bible study for individuals and small groups. The Faith Family Focus series provides youth and adult curriculum for studying MB core values. Kindred also publishes church resources for congregational nurture and membership classes.

As part of the mandate to function as a coordinating link between boards and agencies of the various levels of our conference in matters of resource development and communication, Kindred publishes resources for the Board of Faith and Life (*Faith & Life Pamphlet Series* and the *Confession of Faith*) and the Historical Commission (*Perspectives on Mennonite Life and Thought* series).

Mennonite Brethren cooperate with the Mennonite Church to produce the family worship manual, *Rejoice!*

Mennonite Brethren publications in their various forms and venues all serve as avenues to inform, nurture and inspire the people in our congregations.

PART THREE

Stories
of Growth

Chapter 9
Canada

A family continually grows and changes. If your extended family is like mine, between the time a family picture is taken and hung on the wall, someone has married, a baby has been born or someone has died.

The early MB leaders in North America had a spiritual vision for the denomination. They initiated a church paper, endorsed higher education ventures, and were deeply concerned about maintaining high standards of Christian life and discipleship. Missions, both home and abroad, particularly ignited their passions (see chapter 7). As the denomination grew, as people moved and as demographics shifted, carrying out the spiritual vision of the larger MB family led to ongoing organizational adjustments.

In 1909, for example, Mennonite Brethren in Canada and the U.S. were divided into four district conferences—Northern in Canada and Southern, Central and Pacific located in the U.S. Congregations in these regions worked together to support foreign missions, a seminary, colleges and Bible schools, evangelism, Christian education and publications.

In 1945, the Northern District, which had reached about the size of the other three combined because of Mennonite immigration to Canada, incorporated itself as the Canadian Conference of MB Churches. In 1959, the districts in the U.S. voted to organize the U.S. Conference of MB Churches. This new structure made church growth and evangelism, youth work, Christian education concerns, stewardship, and Bible and liberal arts colleges the responsibility of the national conferences. Foreign missions, faith and life matters, seminary training and resource publications became, for the most part, binational concerns and boards to guide these ministries were formed with representatives from both Canada and the U.S. Congregations sent delegates to regularly scheduled conventions at which decisions regarding the ministries were made.

Eventually some viewed this arrangement as cumbersome and it was suggested that one level of organization needed to be removed. So in 1999, it was decided to dissolve the General Conference (binational), formed in 1879, and to let the two national conferences function separately. As this book is being written, then, the North American Mennonite Brethren family is in the midst of significant change.

It takes time for a family to realize the many ways in which it is changed by a birth, death or marriage, and time, too, helps denominational families realize the implications of its decisions. Some have described the emergence of the U.S. and Canadian national conferences as the "growing pains" of a growing denomination while others believe it reflected an increasing emphasis on nationalism. The same has been said of the 1999 vote to dissolve the General Conference. At present, we do best to recognize that time will tell how this recent change will affect the North American MB family.

This chapter tells the story of the Canadian Conference of MB Churches and the next chapter does the same for the U.S. Conference of MB Churches. Both conferences are focusing on church planting in key urban centers. Both are working to integrate transcultural congregations into their regional and national families.

Given the diversity of Canadian and U.S. Mennonite Brethren today, describing a typical Sunday morning worship service is almost impossible. MB worship is Ethiopians breaking into spontaneous dances and shouting as they sing rhythmic melodies punctuated with high trilling, called *ellitas*. It is an orderly Korean-language service, much the same from one congregation to another, marked by good choir music. It is an English-language service that blends contemporary praise and worship songs with well-loved hymns. Worship is Slavic Christians praying loudly and all at one time while kneeling, not sitting, out of respect to God.

In each of the next two chapters, we will look at more recent events that have shaped who the two national conferences are and what they are involved in as they enter the twenty-first century. The national ministries highlighted in these chapters are changing and developing, making these stories a work in progress.

Growth in Spurts

When Christopher and Sandra Cook came to Calgary, Alberta from South Africa, they were looking for Christian fellowship which matched the spiritual vitality they had enjoyed among the evangelicals of Johannesburg.

On their first Sunday in the city, they attended a downtown church which didn't seem to mention the name of Jesus. Then they found an apartment in the northwest part of town, in plain view of Dalhousie Community Church. The Cooks attended Dalhousie, liked what they heard and saw, and have been enjoying the fellowship there ever since.

The Cooks' story highlights a number of opportunities which the growing cultural variety in Canadian cities offers to Mennonite Brethren churches.

The Mennonite Brethren church in Canada began in 1888 as a tiny mission church of 16 members near Winkler, Manitoba. By 2001, it had grown to a family of 233 congregations with a combined total of 33,426 members scattered "from sea to shining sea."

The Canadian Conference experienced growth in spurts during the twentieth century because of waves of Mennonite immigration into Canada. A large number of MBs were among some 20,000 Mennonites from Russia who entered Canada in the 1920s. Numerous MB churches were established as a result. Another wave of some 7,000 Mennonites entered Canada after World War II and again impacted the Canadian MB churches. These immigrants caused the Canadian churches to be less homogeneous than their U.S. counterparts of the same period.

Immigrants brought both positive energy and challenges to the indigenous Canadian MB family. There were often tensions over language, as German gradually had to yield to English. The newcomers also came with an aggressive vision for ministry, however, and a concern for the needs of their children and youth in a new society, which moved the denomination into ventures such as schools, camps and publications, many of which continue today.

After World War II, Canadian MBs also began what historian J.A. Toews called an "urbanization process." The arrival of the immigrants, combined with city mission work, and the decision by many MBs to move from rural communities to the cities prompted a surge in urban church growth in Alberta, British Columbia, Manitoba, Ontario and Saskatchewan. The return of French-speaking missionaries from the Congo in 1960 provided the Canadian Conference with personnel to begin church planting in Quebec. In the 1970s, the conference began planting churches in the Maritimes.

Canadian MBs Embrace Outreach Vision

If immigration shaped the Canadian MB family for much of the twentieth century, the wider evangelical community of Canada strongly influenced its vision for the twenty-first.

Canada is a fundamentally secular country whose large size and small population has encouraged its evangelical churches to cooperate rather than compete. Canada ranks third among the world's nations in land area, but is ninth on a list of the world's 10 most sparsely populated countries. Ninety percent of the population lives within 100 miles of the U.S. border. This atmosphere seems to have reduced barriers between denominations; they "rub off" on one another. This evangelical cooperation has rubbed off on Mennonite Brethren in the areas of evangelism and church planting.

In the early 1990s, a national event called Vision 2000 was initiated among Canada's evangelical denominations to inspire each other towards reaching the unchurched of the nation for Christ. Vision 2000 impacted the Canadian Conference in two ways. The MB Conference was emerging as a leader in the evangelical community and Vision 2000, as well as subsequent national events, helped the denomination mature in this role. Vision 2000 also galvanized the attention of Mennonite Brethren to church planting and prompted the Canadian

Conference Board of Evangelism to set new, aggressive church planting goals.

The 1997 Canadian Church Planting Congress launched a strategy to plant 10,000 new churches by 2015. Many evangelical denominations, including the Mennonite Brethren, made commitments to set goals and restructure for greater effectiveness in church planting. Focus shifted to key urban centers, and in 1998, the conference approved the "Key Cities Initiative" as a primary strategy of the Board of Evangelism. Calgary, Alberta was chosen as the first key city.

In 1999, after months of careful planning and preparation, the Alberta MB Conference and national evangelism boards announced the appointment of four church planters and "Mission Calgary" was launched. The initial church plants focused on four communities and paired each church plant with an established congregation. One church planter worked in northwest Calgary with Dalhousie Community Church serving as a resource; two church planters were recruited to work in southeast Calgary with Sunwest Christian Fellowship Church as a partner; and a third person worked with a small, already established Ethiopian church. That fall, a fifth church planter was appointed to partner with Grace Church, a Cantonese-speaking MB church, with the goal of eventually establishing a Mandarin-language congregation. The goal of Mission Calgary was to plant 10 churches in 5 years.

Michael and Barb were baptized in the Bow River in August 2000. They were the first to become believers in Jesus through The River, the new church plant in southeast Calgary. Michael's parents were among those who witnessed this event. They were visibly stirred as Michael told how an Alpha course with great food and friends answered the questions that stood between him and a personal relationship with Jesus. They heard Barb speak of a small group of women who helped her receive Jesus' grace and offer his forgiveness to those who had hurt her. One month later, Michael's parents invited Jesus to become their Savior and leader. A small stream of hope is becoming a life-giving river.

Toronto is home to 42 percent of the non-white population of Canada, with visible minorities accounting for 54 percent of the city's population, up from 3 percent in 1961. It is estimated that 70,000 immigrants speaking 100 languages from 160 different countries find their way to Toronto annually.

In 2000, Canadian members pledged to "Love Toronto" and Ontario's capital became the second city targeted under the Key City Initiatives. Toronto is currently home to two multi-cultural MB congregations: New Life Christian Fellowship and Evangelical Asian Church, which are also the province's two fastest growing congregations.

Within five years, the Canadian Conference Board of Evangelism and the Ontario MB Conference want to establish five healthy congregations in the greater Toronto area. Given the ethnic make-up of the city, Love Toronto got off on the right foot in early 2001 when Dan and Carol Sileshi were called as the first church planters. Dan was introduced to the Lord by a Mennonite church in Ethiopia and had previous church planting experience in Zimbabwe and Nigeria.

Mohammed walked into The Meadows Community Church in Mississauga, Ontario one Sunday morning. Having come from Pakistan, he was pursuing a new life in Canada for himself and his family. The pastor invited him for breakfast at a place called "Muggs." That morning in "Muggs," Mohammed asked Jesus Christ to be his Lord and Savor. They later joked that Mohammed was "Mugged for the Master" that day. He said, " I always knew God wanted me to come to Canada for some strange reason; I just didn't know what it was!"

Since then Mohammed has been faithfully growing at The Meadows. He is praying that his wife will also commit to Christ when she comes Canada.

Since church planting and church nurture are two sides of the same coin, the Canadian Executive Board also initiated efforts aimed at helping congregations evaluate themselves. They used a program called Natural Church Development (NCD) which maintains that a church that is healthy in eight essential areas will see its membership grow in quantity and quality. A healthy church is characterized by: leadership that empowers others, gift-oriented ministry, passionate spirituality, structures that work, inspiring worship, need-oriented small groups, need-oriented evangelism, and loving relationships.

In the late 1990s, Canadian Conference congregations were asked to complete the NCD church health survey as part of a national strategy designed to focus congregations on local outreach and address church health. When the survey revealed that person-to-person evangelism was a common weakness among Canadian MB congregations, the Board of Evangelism hired an associate director of evangelism to assist church pastors and lay leaders in developing strategies to build stronger lay-driven ministries focused on discipleship and evangelism.

Priorities for Future Ministry

At the start of the twenty-first century, the Canadian Conference identified three priorities. The first is reaching out through church planting and existing congregations. The second is growing healthy congregations using the Natural Church Development survey and provincial conference ministers who are trained NCD coaches.

The third priority is leadership development. The conference is committed to developing a consistent internship program across the provinces that will start and end with the local congregation. Leadership training will involve cooperation with the three Mennonite Brethren supported colleges and MB Biblical Seminary.

Each of the Canadian Conference boards will continue to make its unique contribution to addressing the priorities of the national conference. The conference is headquartered in Winnipeg, Manitoba, with a cluster of staff members in British Columbia and single staff members in Ontario and Quebec. The Executive Board is the top decision-making and vision-casting board and includes executive committee members, chairs of Canadian Conference program boards and the provincial MB conference moderators. Conference senior executive staff are non-voting members.

The **Board of Faith and Life** oversees the theological health of the conference and has worked in the area of refocusing church leaders as part of the NCD approach to church health and growth. It publishes a series of pamphlets on critical topics including homosexuality, divorce and remarriage, lotteries and materialism.

The **Board of Christian Education Ministries** focuses on developing discipled Christians. It seeks to help local congregations strengthen their Christian education programs for children, youth and adults, and develops evaluation tools. The board also sponsors a triennial youth convention and regional youth worker networks, assists in the publication of French-language Christian Education materials and promotes cooperation among all denominational Christian education ministries.

The **Board of Communications** oversees the four Canadian Conference periodicals (*MB Herald, Mennonitische Rundschau, Le Lien, Chinese Herald*) and the Centre for MB Studies in Winnipeg which collects and preserves the archives of the Canadian MB family. The board is also responsible for the Canadian MB presence on the internet/worldwide web.

The growing ministries of Canadian Mennonite Brethren require the financial commitment of its members. The **Board of Management** gives direction to the financial affairs of the national conference. It monitors the Conference Ministries Support Fund and sets investment guidelines for Stewardship Ministries, an agency which allows congregations and individuals to invest funds which are then made available as loans to pastors, conference workers and churches. Annuity endowments and estate gifts also provide financial support to denominational ministries. The board also oversees the work of Christian Press which offers printing services to all conference boards and agencies.

The Canadian Conference story would not be complete without a look at the current challenges it faces. One is growing regionalism. Provincial conferences are growing stronger; some of them are developing ministries that match national ministries. It is only natural that individuals and congregations support local rather than national ministries.

In both the U.S. and Canada, the fastest growing conferences are its most westerly ones. In Canada, the British Columbia MB Conference accounts for half the national conference membership. The number of MB churches in BC doubled in the 1990s, making Mennonite Brethren the largest evangelical non-charismatic denomination in the province. BC provincial leaders hope to double again in the first 10 years of the new millennium—from 103 congregations to over 200.

One other issue seems to be coming to the forefront. As more multicultural and ethnic-specific congregations are brought into the church family, they must be integrated into the denomination. Integrating the large churches that have emerged in some places into the denomination is also a concern.

Provincial Conferences

Our overview of the Canadian Conference concludes with a brief look at each of the provincial conferences. Congregations send delegates to annual provincial conventions to worship, hear reports on provincial ministries and make decisions. For many conferences, the close of the century coincided with their need to evaluate provincial administrative structures and ministries. The following statistics reflect 2001 figures.

The **Alberta Conference** of 25 churches with a total of 2482 members has focused considerable attention on Mission Calgary. The conference has also recently initiated a new administrative structure designed to facilitate better communication within its commissions and between the conference and its churches. The province owns Camp Evergreen near Sundre, which operates year-round. It supports Bethany Bible Institute, together with Saskatchewan MBs. The conference employs a conference minister and is considering the addition of a church extension director. Financially, the conference has recently been blessed in that giving has met and exceeded the budget.

The **British Columbia Conference** congregations, numbering 103 with a total combined membership of 16,579, today worship in 17 languages and hope to add one new language group each year for the next 10 years. Growth in the BC Conference has accelerated over the last 30 years. Thirteen churches were planted in the 1970s, 29 churches in the 1980s, and 49 churches in the 1990s. The conference would like to add another 100 churches in the next 10 years and it anticipates that the majority of those will worship in a language other than English. BC Conference agencies include Columbia Bible College in Abbotsford, Mennonite Educational Institute in Abbotsford, Gardom Lake Bible Camp at Enderby, Pines Bible Camp in Grand Forks and Stillwood Camp and Conference Centre in Lindell Beach. MB Biblical Seminary is a member of the ACTS Consortium and has a campus in Langley. A conference minister, an executive director of church extension, and an administrator serve the conference.

The **Manitoba Conference** with 6091 members has entered the twenty-first century committed to change. Its churches have shifted from being one church with decisions binding on all to being a "conference of churches," where each church determines its level of commitment to joint ministries. In 2001, the conference completed a five-year evaluation process and changed its organizational structure to include a Council of Representatives of three representatives from each of its 35 churches. The conference also affirmed its commitment to four ministries: Missions and Church Extension (MCE), MB Collegiate Institute in Winnipeg, Canadian Mennonite University in Winnipeg, (formerly Concord College) and Family Life Network, a world-wide radio and media ministry headquartered in Winnipeg. MB Biblical Seminary is in discussion with CMU and others about establishing a regional seminary campus in Manitoba. The conference is served by the conference pastor, conference administrator and a MCE director. Other ministries include Simonhouse Bible Camp at Cranberry Portage.

The **Ontario Conference,** numbering 27 churches with a total membership of 4390, has partnered with the Canadian Conference Board of Evangelism to plant churches in Toronto as part of the Key Cities Initiative. Churches are also emerging in other communities. The Leamington congregation and Waterloo congregations have planted daughter churches and a seventh MB congregation has emerged in St. Catharines. Ontario Conference ministries include Eden High School in St. Catharines, Camp Crossroads in Torrance, Bethesda, a ministry to people with developmental handicaps, and Tabor Manor for senior citizens, both located in St. Catharines. A conference minister and director of church extension serve the conference.

Delegates to the 2001 **Quebec Conference** convention took the opportunity to consider their priorities in light of a new conference mission statement. It stated that the goals of the Quebec Conference are to spread the gospel, create harmony within communities, foster knowledge among believers, and honor God through charitable and community work. In coming years, the conference will work to find practical ways to carry out its mission. The conference works with the national conference in church planting. Its other ministries include a theological school, Ecole de Theologie Evangelique de Montreal in St-Laurent, and Camp Peniel in St-Eustache, a summer camp and year-round retreat center. The Quebec conference includes eight churches with a combined membership of 413. A director of development serves the conference.

The **Saskatchewan Conference** includes 30 churches with a total of 3288 members. Like its sister conferences, it includes congregations that have existed for over 100 years as well as those newly planted. The Saskatchewan Conference employs a conference minister and is considering adding a director of church extension in cooperation with the Alberta Conference. It owns two camps: Redberry Bible Camp near Saskatoon and West Bank Bible Camp near Swift Current. It also owns Bethany Bible Institute together with the Alberta MB Conference and Evangelical Mennonite Missions Conference of Saskatchewan.

Because the Canadian Conference Board of Evangelism is charged with planting churches where no provincial or regional conference exists, the national board leads the denomination's church planting activities in **Atlantic Canada**. The denomination has hopes of establishing 10 churches in this region and as of 2001, is halfway there with three congregations in New Brunswick and two in Nova Scotia with a combined total membership of 183.

Chapter 10
U.S. Conference

When Dean and Jeanette Hudgeons of Westport MB Church in Collinsville, Oklahoma, learned that conceiving children would require medical procedures that were not only expensive but had a low success rate, they began looking into adoption. Over the next several years, the couple witnessed God's hand in bringing five children from four different ethnic and cultural backgrounds into their home. They continue to be open to God bringing more children into their family.

As Dean describes how a birth mother releases her child into their care, his three-year-old daughter jumps in. "I don't belong to Mom and Dad," Aunah says emphatically, "I belong to Jesus." Belonging to Jesus is at the heart of how Dean and Jeanette are working to create a single unit made up of diverse parts. "It's fun to explore Africa, Korea and everything else that's part of our children's biological backgrounds," says Dean. "But our spiritual heritage is what's important and that's what we try to highlight."

Like a Hudgeons family portrait, a Mennonite Brethren U.S. family picture taken today includes people from a variety of cultures and ethnic backgrounds. While U.S. MBs once worshiped in only one language, today as many as 14 different languages and dialects are spoken by more than 26,000 U.S. Mennonite Brethren. Like the Hudgeons family, the U.S. conference is ethnically diverse, but the churches share a spiritual heritage. All are children of God with a common confession of faith, a commitment to evangelism, and a willingness to work with one another.

Uncertainty Brings New Vision

Most families go through some tough times financially, and the 1980s were that time for U.S. MBs. Programs and personnel were drastically reduced in a successful attempt to relieve the conference of its increasing debt. In the aftermath of these cuts, there was some uncertainty as to what direction the conference should take.

The answer to the question, "What's next?" came with the realization that the country U.S. MBs call home was changing. People from nations targeted for MB foreign mission work were coming to America. And the U.S., once strongly influenced by Judeo-Christianity, was becoming post-Christian. U.S. MBs felt called to a new kind of mission work—one that targeted their neighbors, both English-speaking and transcultural.

In 1988, the U.S. Conference adopted numeric goals that have guided it into the twenty-first century: the conference would grow to 25,000 members and 180 congregations by the year 2000. Specifically, local congregations were challenged to grow and the districts, with the help of the conference, were to establish a minimum of five new churches per year with 30 of those new churches being started among different ethnic peoples. Leaders would be needed for these new churches. Established congregations were asked to call out and help prepare two percent of their membership for leadership roles in pastoral ministry and missions.

Was the conference successful in meeting these "Vision 2000," goals? Technically no, not in the year 2000. But one year later, in 2001, the U.S. Conference numbered 180 congregations with a total membership of 26,219. Forty-five transcultural congregations had been established, surpassing the goal of 30. Related statistics reveal that Hispanic congregations account for 23 percent of the churches of the U.S. Conference and that the largest U.S. MB congregation is no longer English-speaking—it is Slavic.

Not all news coming into the new millennium was good news, however. While the number of ethnic congregations had grown as hoped, growth in other areas did not meet expectations. Even with a new commitment to church planting in 1994, church planting, often undertaken without a strong nucleus of believers, was difficult and slower going than anticipated.

A leadership shortage also hampered church growth. Some denominational leaders point to the strong commitment of today's young people as a sign that leaders will emerge in time. Alumni of Youth Mission International, a discipleship and mission program for high schoolers and young adults, are finding their way into leadership positions as are the young men and women who have been involved in a number of internship programs sponsored by the educational institutions and the national evangelism board.

For that reason, the U.S. Conference continues to commit most of its financial and human resources to two ministries born from Vision 2000 and aimed at growing the family: Integrated Ministries, launched in 1988 to assist in planting and integrating transcultural congregations, and Mission USA, a church renewal and church planting ministry organized in 1994 that has targeted America's cities. This chapter will give an overview of these two ministries, introduce the other ministries of the U.S. Conference and briefly describe the five districts that currently make up the conference.

Integrated Ministries:
Transcultural Adoptions Bring Growth

The United States is a land of immigrants. That is as true today as it was in the late 1870s when Russian Mennonite Brethren immigrants came to this country. As of 2000, ethnic people groups in the U.S. were growing at six times the rate of the nation as a whole and in California, ethnic people groups are in the majority.

Many of these immigrants are Christians, eager to establish churches. Take Ethiopian immigrants, for example. When the communist regime took over Ethiopia in the mid 1970s, the government targeted the evangelical church for persecution and many Christians were killed. The church went underground and Ethiopian Christians were scattered across the world. Everywhere they went, including the United States, they formed churches. As of 2001, six Ethiopian congregations located in Washington, California, Kansas and Colorado have affiliated with the MBs.

Since its inception in 1988, Integrated Ministries has been instrumental in planting and integrating over 50 congregations of ethnic people groups into the U.S. Conference. As of 2001, 45 groups were still active conference members with more than 18,000 people attending weekly worship services. Integrated Ministries director Loyal Funk found that ethnic congregations choose to affiliate with Mennonite Brethren for primarily three reasons.

First, they agree with the MB confession of faith. Pastor Yury Chernyetsky of Slavic Mission MB Church in Seattle, Washington said the primary reason his congregation joined the MBs was doctrinal similarities.

Second, the MB insistence on a basic confession of faith and a high view of Scripture combined with flexibility regarding worship style is "a comforting stance" for transcultural congregations. Berhanu Waldemariam of the Ethiopian congregation in Bellevue, Washington said, "Since we are an ethnic church, we have our own style of worship. We appreciate that there is no strong push to tell us how to worship. But doctrinally, I have accountability to the Pacific District Conference."

The Mennonite Brethren's strong emphasis on mission is the third reason for affiliation. The hearts of many transcultural congregations straddle their country of origin and the United States and so do their evangelism efforts.

Many new immigrants to America are not believers but are much more open to the gospel here than they were in their homeland. They may find their way to a transcultural congregation because of the social life it offers but often find more. "I lost my country but I found my Savior when I came to America," says one.

The Japan MB Conference fully supports at least two Japanese language congregations in the U.S. in hopes of reaching as many immigrant Japanese as they can. Since 1999, Slavic Mission Church in Seattle, Washington has been broadcasting a weekly television program, "The Power of the Cross," in Washington and California. In early 2001, the congregation expanded this television ministry to Russia with the prospect of reaching six million viewers on Sunday mornings.

Most transcultural congregations share the deep desire of Slavic Mission Church to do mission work in their country of origin. Bethel Ethiopian Church of Seattle, supports a Christian elementary school in Ethiopia established by its pastor. In 2000, the seven MB

Korean congregations, with a total attendance of 700, were sending humanitarian aid to Korea in cooperation with Mennonite Central Committee. Transcultural churches appreciate the network of mission and humanitarian aid services like MCC and MBMS International available to MB congregations.

Over a period of seven years the Slavic/Russian congregations (numbering 20 with over 10,000 people attending weekly services in 2000) planted more than 100 congregations in the former Soviet Union. MBMSI, the North American denominational mission agency, has partnered with Slavic congregations in some of these projects.

While the U.S. Conference can credit much of its numeric growth to the work of Integrated Ministries, truly integrating transcultural congregations into the denomination is a challenge. They are on track to becoming a large portion of the U.S. Conference, and as they become more integrated, they will no doubt change more than just the ethnic face of the denomination.

Progress towards integration is being made, locally, regionally and nationally. Some church facilities are shared by several MB congregations of different cultures. Joint worship services, gym nights and fellowship meals give the members of these congregations the opportunity to learn to know one another.

The Butler Avenue MB Church in Fresno, California encompasses four congregations: two English language, one Spanish and one South East Asian. Several times a year all four congregations gather at nearby Fresno Pacific University for a joint worship celebration and meal. While participants don't all speak the same language or appreciate the same worship style, the common worship experience transcends cultural and language differences and joins everyone in a common language of the heart.

Those who have formed working relationships and personal friendships with a brother or sister from another culture hope that more members of the Mennonite Brethren family will have the opportunity to do so. True integration at the corporate level will be achieved when we bond with one another at the personal level.

Mission USA—"To Win Some"

The goals set by the U.S. Conference in 1988 called for 50 percent growth by 2000, to consist of a modest increase in membership among existing churches, the adoption of immigrant congregations and the planting of new churches. In the early 1990s, a cross section of U.S. denominational leaders came to an unprecedented decision: they would pool their resources to evangelize the U.S.

The Board of Evangelism and Christian Service was dissolved and a new board, Mission USA, was organized to do whatever it took to "win some." Some aspects of the plan initially proved to be unrealistic. Cooperation among educational institutions and other denominational agencies, for example, while good on paper, was difficult and at times funding concerns took over the vision. In spite of this, the Mission USA commitment to reaching lost people in the neighborhoods and communities of suburban America has remained unchanged.

Mission USA's goal to reach the lost is two-legged: church renewal and church planting. The strategy is developing partnerships with district conferences and local congregations. The writer of Ecclesiastes says, "A cord of three strands is not easily broken," and Mission USA agrees: double and triple partnerships are hard to beat.

Because Mission USA believes that church health is important in achieving church growth, it has given growing attention to church renewal. It helps congregations renew their commitment to evangelism and discipleship in primarily two ways: providing self-study resources to help congregations refocus their ministry and providing funds for a limited number of congregations looking for short-term help of staff and/or resource materials. While taking a long and hard look at themselves is not always comfortable, many congregations report that the self-study used with the Natural Church Development approach (described in the previous chapter) has helped them become healthier congregations.

Partnerships are especially important when planting churches. Mission USA's involvement varies with each church plant as to the church planting strategies employed. In any case, Mission USA hopes to give each new congregation the DNA for evangelism that will make it possible for them to give birth to other congregations, continuing the cycle of growth.

At the heart of Mission USA's current vision is MetroNet 2005, an ambitious plan to plant a total of 20 churches in major metropolitan areas in five years. Mission USA hopes to achieve its goal by planting a cluster or family of churches in a city and expecting some of those plants to birth new churches within a five-year period.

Phoenix, Arizona has been targeted by Mission USA and the Pacific District Conference as the site of the Mission USA headquarters as well as a key city in MetroNet 2005. Copper Hills Community Church was planted in 1997 and within three years had become a self-supporting, free-standing Pacific District congregation. It has partnered with Mission USA and others in planting the next MB church, to be located in northwest Phoenix. Phoenix was selected as the first MetroNet 2005 target city in part because the sprawling desert metropolis of 2.7 million is on its way to becoming the fifth largest city in the nation. It is also a city where only three percent of the population are in church on Sunday morning.

Other urban centers considered as potential MetroNet 2005 target cities are Bellingham, Washington; Minneapolis, Minnesota; Omaha, Nebraska; Denver, Colorado; Salt Lake City, Utah; Wichita, Kansas; Bakersfield, California; and Tulsa, Oklahoma. Many of these cities have established and growing clusters of MB churches.

Omaha, for example, is currently home to five MB congregations. This network got its start when Faith Bible Church, an inner city congregation that shares its facilities with Iglesia Agua Viva, planted Millard Bible Church which in turn helped, in the 1990s, plant Rolling Hills Church in neighboring Papillon which in turn planted New Life Fellowship in northwest Omaha. The Papillon congregation first met in a building which its members operated as a Christian music store during the week. In 2001, the congregation dedicated its new facility located at an intersection that will one day be the home of a major shopping mall.

"Merge to multiply" was the concept adopted by the Parkside MB Church of Tulsa when the congregation decided to merge with Westport MB Church in nearby Collinsville, Oklahoma. In less than four years that goal was realized when the Southern District Conference partnered with Mission USA and Westport in 2000 to plant a new church in the Tulsa suburb of Broken Arrow.

A number of former Parkside members joined the Community Church of the Heart core group. Those involved are praying that Mennonite Brethren in Tulsa will continue to multiply, forming a cluster of MB congregations.

Another city impacted by Mennonite Brethren is the Salt Lake City metroplex. Pioneer church planters Paul and Jini Robie have seen their Morman neighbors come to a personal relationship with Jesus Christ and be baptized and have led their young church family through the growing pains that come naturally to new Christians and new churches. The lack of an evangelical Christian witness in the Salt Lake City area plus the influence of the Church of the Latter Days Saints have prompted Paul and Jini to describe themselves as "cross cultural" missionaries. As of this writing, the church has an attendance of over 450 and they are working on planting another church in the area.

U.S. Conference Ministries Build the Body

Just as a parent strives to guide a child toward maturity, so the U.S. Conference seeks to build the body of Christ. The various denominational ministries each make a unique contribution to helping lost people come to know Christ and Christians grow in their faith.

The U.S. Conference, headquartered in Hillsboro, Kansas, began a reorganization process in 1998. The decision to disband the General Conference prompted additional changes in 2000.

The **Board of Church Ministries** was broadened to include not only chairs of each of the existing national boards and a representative from each district conference, but also a representative from MBMS International and the newly struck Board of Faith and Life. Additional representatives will be added as bi-national ministries shift to national oversight or as new boards are established. Conference senior level staff members are non-voting members. BCM oversees all conference ministries as the conference in interim.

The U.S. Conference **Board of Faith and Life**, established in 2000 as a result of the divestiture of the bi-national conference, is charged with overseeing the spiritual growth of the denomination.

The **Board of Communications** has focused primarily on the publication of *The Christian Leader*, an English-language monthly magazine. It is exploring other ways in which it can serve the needs of the denomination. One priority has been establishing a U.S. Conference web site. The board has also discussed the need for a national communication strategy and is exploring ways to work with transcultural churches in their communication needs.

The **MB Foundation**, headquartered in Hillsboro, Kansas, is a service agency that manages endowment funds, various life income plans, donor-advised funds and the Ministry Investment Fund. These funds are invested to provide capital for building projects throughout the conference. The foundation also provides an avenue by which Mennonite Brethren can support U.S. Conference ministries through charitable gifts.

The **Board of Trustees** manages the legal and financial affairs of the U.S. Conference. The trustees also monitor health care and life insurance benefits for pastors, review trends in compensation and assist the conference in maintaining appropriate records.

The U.S. Conference is involved with a number of ministries that are not represented at the board level. Among these are U-SERV, a program that matches skilled laborers with congregations with facility needs; the Peace Education Commission, charged with helping the denomination understand God's vision for a *shalom* or peace; and the Youth Commission, a group recruited to plan a national youth convention, usually held every four years.

The U.S. Conference is comprised of five districts, organized along geographic lines, with a single transcultural congregation in New York not affiliated with any district. District ministries are not as program-oriented as their Canadian counterparts and most are carried out by a team of volunteers. Each district has responsibility for pastoral oversight and local faith and life issues.

The **Central District Conference** covers a large territory: Nebraska, South Dakota, North Dakota, Montana, Illinois and Minnesota. It includes 25 churches with a combined total membership of 2384. District priorities include church planting and renewal efforts, an annual youth convention and stewardship resourcing; it employs a district minister. The CDC, together with the Southern District, North Carolina District and Latin America District Conferences, owns Tabor College, located in Hillsboro, Kansas.

The **Pacific District Conference** has a volunteer staff member working in home missions and owns and operates Fresno Pacific University in California.

While both the Southern District and Central District have transcultural congregations, much of the work of Integrated Ministries has taken place in the Pacific District. This regional district, therefore, has a unique set of challenges and opportunities. Some issues are practical—like the allocation of finances and personnel—while others are less tangible, such as building unity and harmony among people groups who do things differently.

The Pacific District currently has two district ministers: one assigned to serve Hispanic congregations and one to serve the remaining churches. The PDC Hispanic Council addresses the specific needs of the various Hispanic congregations and recently bought a camp ground to facilitate discipleship and fellowship. The Pacific District Conference includes 101 congregations in Arizona, California, Washington, Oregon and Utah for a combined total membership of 16,326.

The **Southern District Conference** has a membership of 7010 in 39 churches located in Arkansas, Colorado, Kansas, Oklahoma and Texas. The district employs a district minister and a part-time district youth minister. Priorities include church planting, church renewal using the Natural Church Development approach, annual events for children and youth, and providing support for local church Christian education.

When the Krimmer Mennonite Brethren Conference merged with the U.S. Conference in 1960, 11 predominantly African American KMB congregations joined the U.S. Conference. They form the **North Carolina MB Conference** which currently numbers six congregations and a combined membership of 209. The district celebrated its 100th anniversary in 2000, and today has a strong spirit and growing enthusiasm for church renewal and growth. New, young leadership in the district is working enthusiastically to bring this vision to reality.

The **Latin American MB Conference** is a predominantly Hispanic group of 290, born from mission work initiated by the Southern District Conference. It emerged as a national conference in the 1960s. Its eight congregations, particularly LaGrulla MB Church, have the unique opportunity to work with Youth Mission International, hosting teams of high school students and sponsors who minister across the border in Mexico. In 2000, the LAMB Conference worked with other Mennonite congregations in South Texas to hold their first relief sale for the work of Mennonite Central Committee.

Chapter 11
The International MB Family

By all appearances, this is a typical family gathering—family members of the clan from far and wide eating together, telling stories, sharing concerns, singing, praying and conducting family business. Now the group gathers for their closing supper and as the last-minute meal preparation takes place, people are talking, laughing, gesturing and hugging one another. Their fellowship is so enjoyable that when the table is ready, it takes some time for the group to come to attention.

But this is not a reunion of blood relatives; this is a spiritual family gathering. This is the final night of the first-ever global consultation sponsored in 1999 by the International Committee of Mennonite Brethren. And this meal is not an elaborate dinner provided by waiters. It is the Lord's Supper served by moderators of Mennonite Brethren conferences around the globe.

For many of us, the most exciting family events are those that add members. Weddings involve joyous pageantry as a new family unit covenants to live in love. Love consummated becomes life created, resulting in the celebration of birth. Adoptions promise the joy of choosing, receiving and caring for a child.

But equally exciting are those events that signal nurture, maturing and growing independence—first steps, learning to read, college graduation, a first full-time job, a silver wedding anniversary, and milestone employment years. These events let us know we are growing up.

While Mennonite Brethren are not the largest Mennonite group in North America, as of 1998, with a total of 239,284 members and 20,568 fraternally related members, it is the largest Anabaptist denomination worldwide. As the denomination moves into the twenty-first century, North American MBs are recognizing that the churches planted by missionaries in Asia, Africa, Europe and Latin America have matured. These churches may be the offspring of a North American mission vision but they are now eager to join North Americans at the family dinner table. They want to take ownership, as Anabaptists in their own right.

The formation of the International Committee of Mennonite Brethren (ICOMB) in 1990 was an important event in the process of forming an equal partnership among Mennonite Brethren worldwide. ICOMB is a unique fellowship within the larger Anabaptist community. While other Anabaptist groups meet together internationally every six years during the Mennonite World Conference (MWC) assemblies, ICOMB is an informal gathering rather than a worldwide fellowship. As a fellowship, ICOMB was not organized as a decision-making body, but as one that focuses on communication and unity.

Organizationally, ICOMB is still developing, but it continues to progress in its efforts to unite and serve the global family. Since 1997, ICOMB includes representation from each of the 17 national conferences and that same year each conference began forwarding one percent of its annual income to ICOMB.

In 1999, the historic global consultation—a unique and exciting family gathering—was held in Kansas. National conferences were invited to send a conference leader, a theological educator, a woman's leader and a youth leader. To ensure that each conference could send at least two representatives, travel funds were available to the conferences of economically depressed countries.

Throughout the four-day event, signs of a new level of worldwide cooperation were evident. For example, for the first time since its formation, the ICOMB executive committee elected by the national conference moderators did not include two North Americans nor was English the common language. Takashi Manabe of Japan was elected moderator, Maximo Abadie of Paraguay as vice-chair, Ike Bergen of Canada as treasurer and Harry Janzen of Brazil as secretary. That trend continued in 2000 when

Alexander Neufeld of Germany was elected chair and Rolando Mireles of the U.S. was elected as treasurer.

Some common threads emerged among members of the MB family worldwide during the global consultation. Many of the testimonies emphasized the importance of the missionary work of the denomination. Monika Wimmer of Austria described how, with her hands covered with bread dough, she first recognized her need of personal salvation. "In these days I have seen that I am a work of your labor," said Wimmer, who eight years prior had become a Christian thanks to MB missionaries.

Other speakers told of national conference church planting and outreach efforts. The Japan Conference, for example, has a strategy for planting churches in Japan and is committed to sending missionaries to other Asian countries. After describing the struggles experienced by his small congregation, Pastor Jyunichi Fujino said, "I ask those of you who sent missionaries to us, to now pray for us."

While the celebration of evangelism past and present was evident, there was a strong call for personal and corporate renewal based on a commitment to the Anabaptist vision.

In the opening address, Miguel Forero of Colombia said, "Those who have always been in a family do not know what it means to not have one. In the same way, those who have always had good doctrine do not know what it is like not to have it. I am referring to how valuable the Anabaptist doctrine is for me and my brothers and sisters who come from a religious background but not a Christian one. We have found a hope that we can live for and we want to maintain (Anabaptist doctrine) pure and spotless."

Now at the start of a new century, ICOMB is in the process of discerning the core beliefs that its members share. "In order to become one in spirit, it's very important to share a common essence on what we believe from the Bible," says Takishi Manabe, of Japan and a former ICOMB chair. A summary of shared beliefs will not take the place of faith confessions within national conferences, say ICOMB members, but it will foster unity and give the conferences a stronger voice in the global family.

ICOMB is also organizing regional consultations; one took place in 2001 in southern South America and another is planned in the Congo. ICOMB also hopes to establish a web site with links to national conferences.

The remainder of this chapter offers a brief description of the worldwide MB family.

Africa: Angola and Congo

The Angola Mennonite Conference (IEIMA) has entered the new millennium focused on renewing its corporate ministries after a period of some neglect. The IEIMA held its first general assembly in almost a decade in December 2000. Forty people attended the assembly, held in the capital city of Luanda.

The delegates focused on evaluating the work of the church from 1992 to 2000 in the areas of evangelism, finance, development, youth and women's ministries. Hopes emerged for reviving the Bible and missiology school that had closed.

The IEIMA continues to deal with issues of past conflict, integrating lay leadership into the decision-making process and collaborating with North American agencies, Mennonite Central Committee and MBMS International, in ongoing development and mission work.

The Congo MB Conference has appointed, in conjunction with MBMSI, a missionary couple to Angola. Unfortunately, it has been difficult to acquire long-term visas. Pastor Masolo says, "Our ministry in Angola will involve bringing the good news and messages of justice and peace to the MB conference (of Angola), and to assist church leaders in administration and implementation of evangelical programs."

The desire of Congolese MBs to reach out to their African neighbors typifies their joyful faith and service amid a history of civil war, political corruption and economic devastation.

"We live in a developing country—and the church shares the problems," says Leonard Lumeya, an MB lawyer from Kinshasa. "All are affected here."

In spite of those problems, the church is growing. Church buildings are primitive but crowded with worshipers. Suffering is pervasive but the singing is celebratory. The country wallows in a perpetual tale of woe, but members' testimonies ring with perseverance and gratitude. Why?

"This period has enabled the gospel to enter hearts that had been closed before," says Muaku Kinana Sosay, an MB leader in the

Kinshasa region. "When someone has lost hope, they are open to listen to God. People had hope in (former President) Mobutu and our leaders. We found we couldn't put our trust in people. We must put our trust in God."

"And others," adds Muaku. "We live a community life," he says. "The church becomes extended family for the believer" (Christian Leader, November, 1997).

The MB Conference of Congo (CEFMC) traces its roots to the pioneer work of Aaron and Ernestine Janzen in the Bandundu region beginning around 1920. By 1960, 70 MB missionaries operated out of seven centers. Some 6000 believers had been baptized and churches were organized. Various schools including a Bible institute, two hospitals and several dispensaries were also in operation.

When the country became independent of colonial rule in 1960, the evacuation of all missionaries forced local CEFMC leaders to assume a level of administrative responsibility for which they had little training. The new leaders initially struggled in their inexperience but they persevered.

Today the CEFMC numbers almost 350 congregations, divided into three regions, including the Kwilua and Kwango areas of the Bandundu region and the city of Kinshasa. Other key centers are located in Kenge, Bandundi, Kajiji and the Bateke Plateau. The denomination is headquartered in Kikwit.

The CEFMC operates with very little foreign assistance; MBMS International funds are focused on leadership training and social ministries. The lack of significant North American support is an issue, given our affluence and their great need. While some older Congolese church leaders nostalgically envision help coming as in the past, a new generation is more interested in forging partnership connections to provide technical assistance with development projects and personnel with expertise in areas such as health, youth ministry, urban evangelism and Muslim ministry. Both MBMS International and local CEFMC leaders are working toward such partnerships.

Asia: India, Japan, Indonesia and Thailand
India is the oldest MB sister church with non-European ethnic roots. Birthed by the first MB missionaries, Abraham and

FAMILY MATTERS

Maria Friesen of Russia, the Mennonite Brethren Church in India was officially organized on January 4, 1891. A steady stream of missionary nurses and doctors, teachers, evangelists and pastors from North America nurtured the church. Single women missionaries, notable among them pioneer medical doctor Katharina Schellenberg, were especially significant in roles of healing, teaching and evangelizing. Located around the city of Hyderabad in the southern state of Andhra Pradesh, the church was established through the traditional means of the mission "station." These compounds that included churches, hospitals, schools, farming operations and missionary residences were centers for ministry to poverty-stricken "untouchables" (outcastes or *dahlits* as they are now known).

By 1970, changing mission policy (see chapter 7) and rising nationalism combined to allow the India MB church to emerge to autonomous adulthood. Although some of the former mission stations provide facilities for education and medical mission, congregation-centered ministry now characterizes the Indian church. The Indian church is organized in 11 district conferences. Although North American assistance is needed to finance educational and medical institutions, the MB Church of India administers an extensive evangelistic program, pastoral training schools, the network of churches, and cooperative ventures with other Christian denominations. In 1999, the MB Church in India numbered 92,993 members in 837 congregations.

Perhaps the best insight into the church of India is its people. One Indian believer is Mother Jeevamma, a caste Hindu who lived with her husband in the village of Narsarlapally. She first heard about Jesus when Peter, an MB evangelist, came to her village. Jeevamma had severely infected gums which caused her constant, intense pain. She had already lost all her teeth as a result of the infection. Peter asked her ("scolded," she said) why she did not ask Jesus to heal her. That night she prayed, saying that if Jesus would heal her mouth she would believe in him. The next morning her mouth was healed. The pain was gone. Subsequently, she went about the village telling others to believe in Jesus. A number also became Christians. Her husband said he was too old to change his religion and died without becoming a believer.

Once a month, Jeevamma would take the bus to the MB Church in Deverakonda when they celebrated the Lord's Supper. In time, she decided that her own village should have a church. The village elders granted her a small plot of ground across from the well, in the center of the village. She then went to the other villagers, both Christians and Hindus, asking for contributions. She knew the residents, so would ask one person for a bag of cement or two, another for money to buy a certain number of stones, each according to their worth. When the church was completed, all the important people of the village were invited for the dedication. These people, says Werner Kroeker who tells the story, pretty much took over the proceedings, though Jeevamma sat in the service and periodically offered verbal advice on how things should be done—especially during the Lord's Supper and the baptism which were part of the event. By June 1999 when Jeevamma died, the church had grown to 50 members and was served by local elders.

The MB family includes the church in the Asian countries of China, Japan and Indonesia. Mennonite mission work to China began in 1901, eventually penetrated at least four distinct fields, and included cooperative inter-Mennonite mission agencies. Although the MB mission once committed its largest force to China, political events in the 1940s produced an almost total eclipse of information about the church for half a century. Recent reports indicate that tens of thousands of spiritual descendants of the first MBs in China confess Christ as Lord.

The church in Japan began with the compassionate ministry of Mennonite Central Committee after World War II. Centered in the metropolis of Osaka, the Japanese MB church is highly organized, operating their own seminary, youth and camping programs, and supporting fulltime pastors in most of the 15 congregations.

In Indonesia, MBs have very close relations with the Mennonites of the Muria Synod, partly because MB missionaries served in the role of pastoral development among Indonesian Mennonites from 1976-1987. The Indonesian church has been evangelistically aggressive in the face of ethnic and religious violence.

Europe and the Former Soviet Union: Spain, Bavaria, Germany and Austria

After four centuries, Mennonites from America—spiritual heirs of the sixteenth century Anabaptists—returned to Europe. They came to Germany, Austria and other Western Europe nations as agents of reconciliation and ministers of relief with Mennonite Central Committee after World War II. This opened the door for evangelism and church planting by Mennonite Brethren.

In Germany, Neuwied on the Rhine became the first center for outreach and a congregation of mostly East German and Eastern Europe refugees was planted. As that congregation grew, it planted other congregations. That tradition continues today.

In the mid 1990s, the Neuwied congregation sent a couple to Vlore, Albania, as church planters. When war broke out in the Balkans, the congregation established a refugee camp there and helped care for about 2000 war refugees from Kosovo. Every two or three weeks, truck transports would leave the church for the camp. Other congregations and church related organizations used the channels of the Neuwied church to aid the refugees.

In Austria, MCC relief, rehabilitation and reconstruction work following World War II began around Linz, the capital of Upper Austria. From Linz the outreach extended to other cities, including Wels where missionaries Lawrence and Selma Warkentin planted a church. Leadership of that congregation was soon transferred to the first national pastor among the European MB church plants and the Warkentins moved on to another location.

Lawrence and Selma were still in Germany almost 50 years later for the arrival of a new century and a new thrust in church planting. Today, German Mennonite Brethren are committed to planting churches in the former communist East Germany. A church has been planted in Dresden and in 2001 the emerging Berlin church was given official legal status.

The region's history, culture and geography have contributed to the formation of several MB conferences. The *Arbeitsgemeinschaft Mennonitischer Bruedergemeinden in Deutschland*, the first conference established in 1966, is a child of North American MB missionary involvement in Austria. South Germany congregations were initially part of the Austrian conference. The national border prompted them to become an independent body in 1986.

In the late 1970s, *"Aussiedler"*—Mennonite immigrants from the USSR—began arriving in Germany in large numbers. Some joined existing MB congregations but most established their own Mennonite Brethren, Mennonite and Baptist churches. In 1989 a group of these congregations formed the *Bund Taufgesinnter Gemeinden*.

Germany's Anabaptist community also includes a large number of Russian German immigrants who came to Germany in the 1990s and wish to remain culturally Russian German. It is estimated that there are about 250 such congregations in the Anabaptist tradition with some 80,000 members in Germany. Within this group, there are independent MB churches, some with as many as 800 members and 1500 in attendance.

In other European countries, church planting efforts in Spain have resulted in a national conference comprised of one congregation. MBMS International is currently involved in church planting work in Portugal.

Latin America: Brazil, Paraguay, Uruguay, Colombia, Peru, Panama, Mexico and Venzuela

Mennonite Brethren refugees from Russia first arrived in South America in 1930, settling in both Brazil and Paraguay. In Brazil, the German-speaking immigrants established agricultural colonies, then began church extension among their Brazilian neighbors, notably in Curitiba and Santa Carva state. MBMS International mission work in São Paulo and several other states resulted in a Portuguese speaking MB conference in 1967. The German- and Portuguese-speaking conferences merged in 1995. Together they train church leaders through a theological institute/seminary.

In Paraguay, the settlers joined Canadian Mennonite emigrants to establish five German-speaking colonies. The Paraguayan MB church has actively evangelized among Indian tribes and in Asunción and other cities through the Evangelism Explosion program. The result has been the formation of two MB conferences, one using German and the other Spanish. The Paraguayan church has established a network of institutions, including camping programs and theological training programs. Although German is still the language of choice in the colonies, Spanish predominates in the churches and institutions of the cities.

Through outreach from Paraguay, an MB church has been planted in Cordoba, Argentina.

MB mission work in Colombia began in 1945 among Indian tribes. Since 1958 churches have been established in the cities of Cali, Medellin and Bogota. Despite earlier periods of persecution and more recent violence due to drug-related gangs, the church in Colombia is active in evangelism and theological training. Mission work in Peru, which Krimmer Mennonite Brethren missionaries began in 1950, has produced churches among Ashaninca Indians, and since 1984, an MB conference in the northern cities of Piura and Sullana. In Panama, literacy work among Choco Indians begun in 1953 produced a small group of congregations associated with Mennonite Brethren though known locally as The United Evangelical Church.

In Mexico, mission work begun in the 1950s has produced a small cluster of congregations associated with Mennonite Brethren that calls itself the Christian Peace Church of Mexico. In addition to the congregations in Guadalajara and Leon, MBMSI cooperates with other Anabaptists in church planting work in Mexico City.

Pancho, a Mexican construction laborer, tells of his encounter with Christ. "When Pastors Enrique and Manuela first came to my home to give Bible studies to my wife, I usually left the house to go out for alcohol or drugs. Even though I had four small children at home, I would rather spend the few coins I found in my pocket on my chemical vices than on caring for them. Eventually, my wife committed her life to Christ. The change in her was dramatic. Because of her prayers and the kindness of the pastoral couple, I began to attend the Bible studies myself. I saw that I needed to change and that only Christ could change me. The moment I committed my life to Christ, I lost all desire for the chemicals that had ruled my life. Even though I have limited means and education, I seek to give service to the church of Mexico." Pancho's story typifies the story of the Latin American church.

Through the efforts of the Chinese MB churches in Vancouver, British Columbia, two Chinese MB churches have been formed in Venezuela.

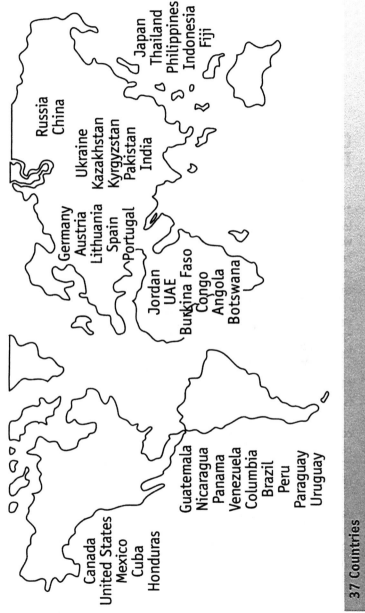

Russia
China

Ukraine
Kazakhstan
Kyrgyzstan
Pakistan
India

Japan
Thailand
Philippines
Indonesia
Fiji

Germany
Austria
Lithuania
Spain
Portugal

Jordan
UAE
Burkina Faso
Congo
Angola
Botswana

Canada
United States
Mexico
Cuba
Honduras

Guatemala
Nicaragua
Panama
Venezuela
Columbia
Brazil
Peru
Paraguay
Uruguay

37 Countries
800 Workers
17 National conferences

Chapter 12
Inter-Mennonite Connections

Kathleen Hartzler and her family were busy August 23, 1992, putting up storm shutters, trimming trees and bringing loose objects inside their home. Hurricane Andrew was on its way and, according to television news reports, the eye was headed directly at them, never wavering. The intensity of the storm kept building—winds were reported at 125 miles per hour, then 145 and finally 165.

The family was also busy answering the phone. Friends and neighbors wondered about their plans—would they evacuate? "If this phone wouldn't ring, we could finish getting ready," Kathleen thought.

"But there was one very welcome call," Kathleen recalls, "from Mennonite Disaster Service: We'll be there when the storm is over" (Detweiler, 275-6).

When the storm was over, MDS volunteers arrived and kept coming for almost two years as they helped a steady stream of people rebuild their homes and their spirits. With damage totaling $25 billion, Hurricane Andrew proved to be the worst disaster (as of 1999) in terms of property damage in U.S. history.

A total of 4250 MDS volunteers gave a total of 27,825 workdays to the folks of Florida and another 2350 volunteers spent a total of 14,200 workdays in neighboring Louisiana. While these volunteers aided Kathleen and others from Homestead Mennonite Church, they also gave their time and energy to helping people who had never seen or heard of Mennonites.

One such person was an elderly man named Ed. After Hurricane Andrew, the lists of those referred to MDS for assistance were long; it often took weeks to assess all the cases and to offer aid. Ed was glad when MDS construction foreman Chris Eash finally got to his house.

Ed went to the bedroom, dug into a full closet and pulled out a shoebox containing $11,000. He had received a Federal Emergency Management Agency (FEMA) check for the damage to his home. Trusting neither FEMA nor the bank, he had cashed the check immediately and put his money in the shoebox. With great relief, he handed the $11,000 to Chris. He had found someone he could trust, he said, and now could sleep at night (Detweiler, 82).

Helping Hands

To be part of the Mennonite Brethren family is to be part of the larger Anabaptist family tree. "Our family is God's way of taking really good care of us," is a familiar sentiment and one that fits the larger Mennonite family. To be Mennonite Brethren is to know that when calamity strikes a member of this extended family, the rest of the Anabaptist family will come to your aid. It is to know, further, that assistance is extended not only to other family members but also to needy strangers "in the name of Christ."

Mennonite Disaster Service (MDS), established in 1950, is probably the most "grassroots" of all inter-Mennonite agencies. MDS is a bi-national (Canada and the U.S.) agency that responds to disasters in these two countries on behalf of many Mennonite and related groups. Except for a small staff at headquarters in Akron, Pennsylvania, and a regional office in Winnipeg, Manitoba, volunteers make up the entire network. Local units are grouped into regions and each region has its volunteer leadership. MDS cooperates with other church and disaster response groups including the American Red Cross and The Salvation Army. MDS works in close cooperation with the Federal Emergency Management Agency and its state counterparts in the U.S. and the Emergency Measures Organization in Canada.

MDS is recognized among inter-Mennonite agencies as having the widest diversity of constituent support. Old Order

Mennonites, Beachy Amish, Mennonite Church, Mennonite Brethren, Brethren in Christ, Conservative Mennonites and others wear the MDS badge. When Hurricane Hugo struck South Carolina in 1989 over 7000 MDS volunteers helped with recovery efforts. Frank McCoy, pastor of Pinopolis (SC) United Methodist Church, shares this story:

"One evening a small slim Amish man with a long gray beard, black felt hat, homemade clothes and suspenders came up to me. He said, 'People around here think we are peculiar.'

"I looked him up and down and blurted, 'You are.'

"He was startled, so I quickly added, 'You've left your homes, families, friends and all that's familiar. You've never met us before and probably never will again. Yet here you've come hundreds of miles from home to work on other peoples' houses in Moncks Corner. You work from sunup to sundown without pay. You bring your own tools. If we can't supply the material you need, you furnish it yourself.

'You ask nothing in return. It seems to us that all of you are working in the way Jesus would if he was here in this mess. Yes, we do think you MDS workers are peculiar'" (Detweiler).

What a privilege—to be considered "peculiar" because we Mennonites, Amish and like-minded Christians have a biblical understanding of faith that embraces a community of caring for each other and our neighbors. The Anabaptists of the sixteenth century cared for others and their descendants, the Mennonites, have never been able to escape this heritage. In Europe, in North America and around the world, Mennonites have committed themselves again and again to service in Jesus' name.

Why? Because we Mennonites believe that authentic faith is expressed in every dimension of life. One recurring theme of Menno Simons was that true faith should "bear fruit." In his classic words, "True evangelical faith...cannot lie dormant, but manifests itself in all righteousness and words of love:...it clothes the naked; it feeds the hungry; it comforts the sorrowful; it shelters the destitute; it aids and comforts the sad."

Serving the Needs of Others
North American Mennonites first rallied together in 1920

when a delegation of Mennonites from Russia visited North America. Mennonites in Russia were facing extreme hardships from the political upheaval and extreme drought in their country and they appealed to their brothers and sisters on this continent for assistance. North American Mennonites responded in two ways: providing relief aid and assisting with immigration.

Mennonites in the U.S. formed a united relief agency, Mennonite Central Committee. A Mennonite Brethren from Hillsboro, Kansas, P.C. Hiebert, was chosen to lead the fledgling agency. Under MCC, Mennonites in Canada and the U.S. raised $1 million and sent three American workers to deliver aid to Russian and Ukrainian villages. Food kitchens were established and tractors sent to help with land cultivation.

In Canada, the Canadian Mennonite Board of Colonization was formed in 1922 to assist the Russian Mennonites emigrate and resettle in Canada. Its first task was to lobby the Canadian government for permission for Mennonites and other conscientious objectors to enter the country. Permission was granted and over 18,000 Mennonites re-located to Canada between 1923 and 1927. About 25 percent were Mennonite Brethren.

As the Mennonite population in Canada grew, so did the various agencies organized to aid the immigrants and the Canadian Mennonite family as a whole. In 1963, six inter-Mennonite agencies agreed to merge and MCC Canada was born. This new organization avoided an overlapping of services, promoted efficiency and presented a united witness.

Inter-Mennonite cooperation embraced a new cause in Canada and the U.S. during World War II. Mennonites in both countries had to face a national draft, and thanks to the efforts of leaders from the historic peace churches, conscientious objectors (COs) were given the option to perform civilian alternative service work of "national importance."

Records are not clear on how many of the 11,000 postponements granted in Canada for reasons of conscience against military involvement went to Mennonites but one source suggests 7500. In the U.S., 12,000 men, including 7000 Mennonites, Amish and Brethren in Christ, registered as conscientious objectors. Many Mennonite COs would have preferred to do relief work in wartorn countries, but national policy did not allow for overseas work by conscientious objectors. In 1941, Alternative Service Work camps were established in five Canadian national parks where the men worked at fire fighting, highway construction, fencing, telephone lines, bridge building, mine props, logging and gravel hauling. Two years later, CO work assignments were expanded to include service in agriculture and industry.

In the U.S., Civilian Public Service (CPS) workers built roads, fought forest fires, constructed dams, planted trees, built contour strips on farms, served as "guinea pigs" for medical and scientific research, built sanitary facilities for hookworm-ridden communities, and cared for people with mental illnesses and juvenile delinquents.

"This movement of young men (and volunteer women) from a wide variety of Mennonite groups into service camps has probably had a more profound effect on North American Mennonites than any other single experience," says Lowell Detweiler, MDS director from 1986 until 1998. "Once the 'quiet in the land,' Mennonites began to look outward for service ministries" (Detweiler,32).

During the years following World War II, MCC expanded its service programs both in North America and around the world. The agency had served its constituency well as a wartime service agency and now converted its organizational capabilities to serving ongoing peacetime needs. With the closing of the CPS program, MCC had experienced, young leaders ready to go to work. The men returned home from alternative service camps with a new zeal and devotion for work in the church and community. Many Mennonite Brethren participants found their way to Bible school or Bible college and became leaders in the MB Church. They were committed to serving others and other inter-Mennonite organizations were born, including MDS.

One area to which Mennonites gave their attention was mental health. During WW II, CPS workers assigned to mental health institutions found the hospital situations desperate. Eventually, American conscientious objectors who had worked in the hospitals of 22 states shared their observations with the public to help effect reforms. Based on the documentary evidence gathered over four years by CPS men, the May 6, 1946 issue of *Life* magazine exposed the deplorable state of affairs. The article said: "Through public neglect and legislative penny-pinching, state after state has allowed its institutions for the care and cure of the mentally sick to degenerate into little more than concentration camps on the Belsen pattern."

In some situations, CPS men influenced practices at state hospitals by reforming them. In most cases, the Mennonite CPS units in a state hospital are not remembered for their focus on reform, but as people who did an honest day's work and had a genuine interest in the patient.

"No other church group had ever had such a concentrated experience with mental illness as the American Mennonites during World War II," said Elmer M. Ediger, a former CPS volunteer who went on to serve as CEO of a Mennonite mental health hospital before his death. "During a four-year period 1,500 Mennonites had a 'hands on' involvement with mental illness which they shared freely with their home congregations. They developed a vision of what might be done with rightly motivated psychiatric aids and mental health professionals" (Neufeld).

Mental health became a rallying cause among Mennonites after WW II. In 1947, MCC began its own mental health program. By 1967, MCC had established seven mental hospitals in the U.S. and one in Canada, and Mennonite Mental Health Services was formed as a subsidiary of MCC to oversee these institutions. Today these hospitals are independent community services and Mennonite Health Services supports not only mental health centers but also retirement communities and developmental disabilities programs in North America and helps to link these agencies to Mennonite, Mennonite Brethren and Brethren in Christ churches.

Defining the ministry of MCC today is like the seven blind men who tried to describe an elephant by feeling a different part of its body—every part is unique and important, but the sum of the animal is greater than the individual part. MCC is an agricultural worker in Bangladesh and a social service worker in Texas. It is an administrator on the scene of an earthquake in India and an accountant in the home office.

MCC is the worker who sat with Carmen Amalia in the ruins of her home in La Florida, El Salvador. Carmen had just stepped into her adobe home and greeted her grandchildren on January 13, 2001, when the ground began to shake. Her bad limp made the few steps to the door impossible. Carmen gathered her two small grandchildren into her arms and prayed as the walls of her house crumbled around her.

"That we are here alive is a miracle from God," Carmen told the MCC worker who visited her 11 days after the catastrophe that left 10 percent of the Salvadoran population homeless.

"I was really scared for days. I couldn't forget [the experience] for a moment. With each new tremor, I thought it was another earthquake. It's not until now that I've begun to eat a little" (MCC News Service Report).

La Florida is a rural community of some 20 families who have transformed an old-style Salvadoran plantation into a farming cooperative. Needs are great after the earthquake. Since a disproportionate number of homes built with traditional adobe bricks were affected by the quake, Carmen and her neighbors no longer trust adobe. But cement block is beyond their means.

Media and relief attention is focused on a neighboring urban community which was buried under a landslide. But thanks to La Florida's connection to a local development organization that partners with MCC, funds are on their way. MCC has a history of working with its local partners in communities that are often forgotten in massive relief efforts.

The many decisions to be made after a disaster—who receives aid, how much and in what form—are delicate ones for communities like La Florida. They require a solid base of experience, trust and dialogue with the community. Local agencies have the necessary base of relationships to ensure that reconstruction does not become a source of division. For this reason, MCC often chooses to channel relief and reconstruction funds through its partner agencies.

MCC also partners with other inter-Mennonite agencies to meet the needs of people around the world. For example, in 2001 MCC and Mennonite Economic Development Associates (MEDA) were at the midpoint of a five-year $7.5 million poverty alleviation project in China. MEDA was begun by North American Mennonites in 1953 to help Mennonite immigrants living in the Chaco region of Paraguay. And as is the case with many of the Mennonite "in-house" projects, MEDA has matured into an agency that is involved in worldwide economic development.

In China, MEDA and MCC are working together with the Canadian International Development Agency and the Amity Foundation, the only Christian-based non-governmental organization in China. The project has four thrusts: agricultural production and marketing; basic health, nutrition and gender equity; basic education and literacy; and economic diversification, including micro-finance.

MBs Contribute to World Relief

Mennonite Brethren support MCC in a variety of ways. Mennonite Brethren volunteer as MCC workers for both short and long term assignments. Historically we have a smaller percentage of MCC workers than other Anabaptist groups.

MBs have been involved in initiating and staffing thrift shops that sell recycled goods to raise funds for MCC. Some thrift shops also sell crafts marketed by Ten Thousand Villages, a division of MCC that markets handmade arts and crafts in North America. Ten Thousand Villages creates the equivalent of 12,000 fulltime jobs yearly for Third World artisans in more than 30 countries. In some communities Mennonite men have banded together to sing and use their concerts to raise awareness and dollars for the cause. Mennonite Brethren also collect items for the school bags, newborn kits and hurricane buckets distributed to needy individuals.

In 2001, MBs in South Texas joined with other Mennonite churches to initiate one of the newest of 45 MCC relief sales. More than $3 million dollars earmarked for MCC are raised annually through these sales. MCC relief sale auctions usually begin with the selling of a loaf of bread. In South Texas, the first item auctioned was a dozen homemade tortillas.

A Family of Faith

Homemade tortillas and mariachi bands at MCC relief sales along with Brunswick stew and Ethiopian *injera* mark another reality for the Mennonite family. On any Sunday you will find over one million Mennonites and related groups gathering for worship in more than 60 countries around the world. The Mennonite church includes a wide variety of people and their practices. For example, in the United States there are at least 46 varieties of Mennonites numbering more than 300,000. This creates many Mennonite images, none complete in itself.

"All of us have to own the great diversity in the Mennonite world," says John A. Lapp, Mennonite educator, historian and the former director of Mennonite Central Committee. "We come from all sorts of different backgrounds and varieties.

"We've created the activist image of Mennonite Central Committee and Mennonite Disaster Service. We've created the cultural and media images of plain peoples. We've created the theological and ethical images of the great minds among us. Now with more Mennonites in Africa, Asia and South America than in North America, we have a new international image. We should be grateful for all the images" (Detweiler, 31).

One snapshot of the larger Mennonite community is the one taken every six years when Mennonites from around the globe gather in one location for a weeklong celebration of kinship in Christ. Mennonite World Conference (MWC), an international communion of Mennonite and Anabaptist-related national conferences with offices in Strasbourg, France, and Kitchener, Ontario, organizes the global celebration.

The first MWC gathering was held in Basel, Switzerland, in 1925 and was attended by representatives from North America, Holland, France and Germany. The thirteenth and most recent MWC assembly, held in 1997, gives witness to the growth of the Anabaptist family. This convention, only the second gathering to be held outside of North America or Europe, was held in Calcutta, India. It was attended by 4472 registrants from 65 countries, with 2942 of those coming from India. Because Mennonite Brethren are the largest group of Mennonites in India, they played an important role in organizing the assembly.

"Since 1994, the majority of our members live in the South," says present MWC executive secretary Larry Miller. "In 1997 in Calcutta we experienced the first Assembly where the new majority was actually present in the majority and articulate spokesmen for that majority were named MWC president (Mesach Kristeya of Indonesia) and vice president (Bedru Hussein of Ethiopia)."

Mennonite Brethren journalist Don Ratlzaff reflected on his experience at India '97 by focusing on the *shamiana*, a tent and bamboo structure erected in India for social and religious events. He describes the *shamiana* as a powerful visual metaphor the global Mennonite family needed to see and experience.

Meeting in a structure where dust, smoke and even the occasional neighborhood dog wandered in freely, rather than in a modern convention center, helped bring home the point that the majority of Mennonites now live in the southern hemisphere. "It should remind us the church is growing most dramatically where the doors not only are open, but in many cases are literally nonexistent," says Ratzlaff.

"From the outside, the worship *shamiana* was a drab canvas brown. Inside, though, the tent came alive with purple and pink fabric," says Ratzlaff. "Seems to me the world too often sees the Mennonite Church from the outside. A functional bunch, they think, but rather colorless and plain. But come inside, where the world gathers, and you will find life, color and spirit" (Christian Leader, February, 1997).

The *shamiana* is also a temporary structure. This symbolizes, says Ratzlaff, the reality that the Holy Spirit does not take up permanent residence. "Yes, the Spirit continues to work in the Mennonite 'homelands' of Europe and North America, but the locus of the Spirit's most dramatic activity has shifted to Asia, Africa and Latin America. We North Americans may have institutions of brick and mortar, but the Two-Thirds World has a church on the move."

Since 1997, MWC has developed a variety of programs that, in addition to the global assemblies, will provide face-to-face fellowship, personal encounters and cooperative experiences among its members. These new activities include a leadership exchange program, a young adult exchange program, a global Mennonite history endeavor, and a program to ascertain global gifts.

Developing a greater mutuality between the churches of the North and South is the challenge facing the Anabaptist family as we enter the new millennium. MWC, together with other agencies, is attempting to guide the process. For too long we in North America have been giving; it is now time to both give and receive.

"Our family has changed greatly as we have grown, added new members and changed color through the 20th century," says Mesach Krisetya. "We need to make room for everyone at the table; the table needs to be extended to make space for the extended family."

Tables

INTER-MENNONITE AGENCIES

Inter-Mennonite agencies are often referred to by acronyms. Here is a list of some of the inter-Mennonite agencies in which Mennonite Brethren are involved. This list is not exhaustive.

Mennonite Central Committee (MCC)
- the relief, service and peace agency of North American Mennonite and Brethren in Christ churches.

Mennonite Disaster Service (MDS)
- a North American disaster relief agency

Mennonite World Conference (MWC)
- a fellowship of Mennonite and Brethren in Christ churches around the world

Mennonite Economic Development Associates (MEDA)
- serves low income people around the world through a business-oriented approach to development

Mennonite Mutual Aid (MMA)
- Anabaptist stewardship ministry

Mennonite Health Services (MHS)
- supports health care agencies by connecting them to Mennonite and Brethren in Christ development.

Meetinghouse
- a cooperating group of Mennonite and Brethren in Christ editors

CIM—Council of International Ministries (CIM)
- a group of North American Anabaptist mission agencies and affiliated overseas ministries.

WORLDWIDE MEMBERSHIP

The 2000 Mennonite World Conference world directory shows that the number of baptized members in 197 Mennonite, Brethren in Christ and related congregations in 63 countries now stands at 1,203,995. That is an increase from the 1998 directory that showed 1,060,143 baptized believers in 192 bodies in 61 countries.

Continent	1998	2000
Africa	322,708	405,979
Asia/Pacific	157,075	184,049
Central/South America and Caribbean	102,496	112,128
North America	415,978	443,918
Europe	61,886	57,9121

The six countries with the most baptized Mennonite and Brethren in Christ members has been the same in 1998 and 2000.

USA	319,768
Congo	183,040
Canada	124,150
India	90,006
Indonesia	87,802
Ethiopia	73,219

Other countries with over 20,000 members in 2000 are Germany, Kenya, Paraguay, Tanzania and Zimbabwe.

PART FOUR

Future Perspective

Chapter 13
The Challenge for the Future

I remember a quirky 60s television show about a family "Lost in Space." In each episode, the family found itself in a strange new world that tested their survival skills. The MB family resembles the "Lost in Space" TV family in some striking ways.

We live in what futurist philosophers are calling "The Postmodern World." The postmodern environment is particularly challenging because it has proven impossible to label (it is the age after "modernism") and difficult to describe. Someone has said that if modernism stood for order, regulation and stability, postmodernism stands for chaos, uncertainty, otherness, openness, multiplicity and change.

The MB family also faces significant change within our denominational structures. This book is being published by the General Conference of Mennonite Brethren churches, a structure that voted itself out of existence in the last year of the old millennium. The General Conference was composed of the MB Church of Canada and the U.S., but ministries have been shifted to the national conferences.

What can we anticipate for the MB Church of the future? What kind of survival skills will we need for the new millennium? What is the new reality?

The notion of postmodernism rests on a philosophy suggested by "deconstructionist" Rene Derrida. According to Derrida and other communication theorists, "ultimate reality" is impossible to know. Each culture "constructs" its own reality by using words, by telling stories. If we as Christians use this terminology, we might say that the search for "Ultimate Reality" (whom we know as God) can be satisfied by finding our place in the "Ultimate Story" (God's saving act through Jesus Christ).

The Christian story makes the claim that the Word Jesus Christ reveals God as the Ultimate Reality. As MBs, we tell our own unfinished story as one expression of the search to truly experience God as the Ultimate Reality. We invite others to claim this narrative as their own story.

In the past, the MB family struggled to define our central story line. We were tempted to use ethnic cultural ties from our Russian past that included our Low German heritage, but that descriptor was not persuasive in a family that includes Telegu speakers in India and French speakers in Congo. Theological distinctives, including both evangelical influences and Anabaptist roots, provide clues for the story line. Perhaps the most succinct way of identifying our story is to speak of the family that lives as a renewal missionary movement. Our renewal is based on a commitment to a New Testament model of the discipling community. Our missionary call invites the world to live under the sovereign rule of God. MBs are those who make this story their own, those who accept adoption into this family in which God is Parent.

The MB story, like the postmodern world in which we seek to find our way, is open-ended. The challenge of the future demands that we consider factors which shape our story. How will our family ties empower us to offer a story that others will find compelling?

Our first challenge is to tell the family story in a way that is both inclusive and distinct. As MBs we are pleased that a strange dialect or head coverings or odd clothes can no longer identify us. We are glad that our churches increasingly welcome members from a rainbow of ethnicities. We have lowered some theological barriers. The Lord's Supper is open to all who claim faith in Jesus, not just baptized believers. We've done our best not to let our "Anabaptist quirks" keep anyone away. We are doing well when we avoid letting nonessentials distance us from fellow worshipers.

Jesus warns against seeking social acceptance, however. He pronounces that those who face persecution for their commitment to God's rule are blessed. To have a story worth telling in our pluralistic world, we will need to continue to center our story on the cross. We will follow Jesus—even at the cost of the death of our reputations and popularity. According to the late Mennonite theologian John H. Yoder, following Jesus can be described as "radical social nonconformity." Our greatest challenge for the future is to choose and learn the lifestyle of the narrow way.

Our family will need proclaimers who can lead us into visualizing, describing and living out the story of God's rule. Leadership committed to "upside-down kingdom" values will be essential to reach the postmodern world. The church must issue the challenge of self-sacrificial servant leadership to its best and brightest—women and men—and be open to having them lead. Anabaptist church leadership is marked by mutuality, involving the community in ministry teams with its pastors.

Worshipping together shapes the story. As we glorify God, we build community and we build faith. Experience and participation are important values in the postmodern world, so our worship must balance fresh experience with tradition. Worship reinforces our corporate identity, offering vital communion with God and the family of faith without succumbing to the siren song that compels us to seek to be novel, innovative and market-driven.

Family ties are demonstrated through distinctive relationships. Jesus said that his family would be identified by the remarkable love they have for each other. A renewal missionary movement expresses love through mutual care. If the Mennonite Brethren movement is to remain vital, it must be marked by sacrificial generosity. Like the modern world before it, the postmodern world lives by the bottom line. Use of money and possessions reveals our most deeply held values. With a global family that is desperately poor, we with western wealth must invest profoundly in the kingdom proclamation of good news for the oppressed.

Finally, the future shape of our family will be determined by how well we maintain our family ties. Love is expressed by fellowship in ever-expanding circles. We are invited to move beyond individual piety to become part of the covenant community that is the church. Congregations partner with others in regional mission. A generation of visionary leaders with a burning passion for the MB world family will lead us into a new partnership of equals with other national conferences. The international MB family will connect with the renewed Mennonite World Conference, led by third world Christians with a heart for evangelism.

Nearly twenty years ago theologian Howard Loewen outlined the MB vision for building family ties. His words still ring true today. He called for

(1) a growing awareness of our Anabaptist-pietist Christian roots;
(2) good news proclamation of Jesus' kingdom for the poor;
(3) spiritual rebirth nurtured by spiritual discipline;
(4) biblical focus on obediently following Jesus; and
(5) kinship with the global family of God.

The Bible verse that Menno Simons placed on the title pages of all his writings is an appropriate benediction for this look at the family that bears his name: "For no one can lay any foundation other than the one already laid, which is Jesus Christ" (1 Cor. 3:11).

Bibliography

Bender, Harold S. *The Complete Works of Menno Simons*. Scottdale, PA: Herald Press, 1956.

Bragt, Thielman J. van. *Martyr's Mirror*. Compiled by Menno Saute, 1944.

Capon, Robert Farrar. *The Parables of Grace*. Grand Rapids, MI: Eerdmans, 1991.

Clapp, Rodney. *Families at the Crossroads: Beyond Traditional and Modern Options*. Downers Grove, IL: InterVarsity Press, 1993.

Confession of Faith of the Mennonite Brethren. Winnipeg, MB: Kindred Productions, 1999.

Confession of Faith Commentary and Pastoral Application. Winnipeg, MB: Kindred Productions, 2000.

Detweiler, Lowell. *The Hammer Rings Hope: Photos and Stories from Fifty Years of Mennonite Disaster Service*. Scottdale, PA: Herald Press, 2000.

Keim, Albert. *The CPS Story: An Illustrated History of Civilian Public Service*. Intercourse, PA: Good Books, 1990

Loewen, Jacob A, and Wesley J Prieb. *Only the Sword of the Spirit*. Winnipeg, MB: Kindred Productions, 1997.

Neufeld, Vernon H. *If We Can Love: The Mennonite Mental Health Story*. Newton, KS: Faith and Life Press, 1983.

Oyer, John S and Robert S Krieder. *Mirror of the Martrys*. Intercourse, PA: Good Books, 1990.

Toews, J.B. *A Pilgrimage of Faith*. Winnipeg, MB: Kindred Press, 1993.

Toews, John B. *Perilous Journey: The Mennonite Brethren in Russia 1860 – 1910*. Winnipeg, MB: Kindred Press, 1988.

Toews, Paul, ed. *Bridging Troubled Waters: The Mennonite Brethren at Mid-Twentieth Century*. Winnipeg, MB: Kindred Productions, 1995.

_____. *Mennonites and Baptists: A Continuing Conversation.* Winnipeg, MB: Kindred Press, 1993.

Wenger, J.C. *How Mennonites Came to Be.* Scottdale, PA: Herald Press, 1977.

_____. *What Mennonites Believe.* Scottdale, PA: Herald Press, 1977.

Works Cited

Chapters 1 and 2

Bender, Harold Stauffer. "A Brief Biography of Menno Simons."
The Complete Writings of Menno Simons. Scottdale, PA: Herald
Press, 1956, 4-29.

Toews, John A. *A History of the Mennonite Brethren Church*.
Fresno, CA: Board of Christian Literature, 1975.

Wenger, J. C. *How Mennonites Came to Be*. Scottdale, PA: Herald
Press, 1977.

Wiebe, Katie Funk. *Who Are the Mennonite Brethren?* Winnipeg,
MB and Hillsboro, KS: Kindred Press, 1984.

Chapter 9

Evangelism Canada, March 1999 and September 2000.

Glossary

Ban – Excommunication or condemnation by the church. The banned individual was not allowed to associate with other church members. In certain cases, even family members were to disassociate with this individual.

Canon – The 66 books of the Bible

Creedalism – A rigid adherence to a creed (statements of belief). The right belief becomes more important than living out the belief in everyday life.

Christian Leader – The periodical of the U.S. conference, published monthly.

Fundamentalism – Religious belief based on a literal interpretation of the Bible and regarded as fundamental to the Christian faith.

General Conference – Governing body for all the MB churches in Canada and the U.S. It met in joint convention biennially and gave governance to faith issues, missions, seminary training and publications.

Global volunteers – Short term programs for adults and youth. Missionaries raise their own support.

Hermeneutic – Interpretation of scripture.

Indigenization – Transfer of missionary run programs to local run programs with the missionaries serving as support and resource.

Just war theory – A primary Christian alternative to nonresistance based on New Testament peace teachings rather than reference to Old Testament war. Criteria is established under which a war should be fought.

MB Herald – The English periodical of the Canadian conference, published bi-weekly.

Muensterite Error – An enthusiastic, fanatical group of Anabaptists who felt they had direct inspiration from God regarding the return of Christ, polygamy and other weird interpretations of scripture.

Multi-term Missionaries Core – Missionaries serve for multiple terms of service (one term is generally three years) and are supported through the MBMSI budget.

Multi-term Missionaries CorePlus – Missionaries serve for multiple terms of service (one term is generally three years) and are supported through personal fundraising.

Partner Workers – National church planters, teachers and evangelists who are supported by MBMS International.

Sacramentalism – Belief in the effectiveness of the sacraments especially the doctrine that the sacraments are necessary to salvation.

Single-term Missionaries Core – Programs of single terms of service (i,e, Church Planter Residency) or shorter terms of service of nine months or more (i.e. TREK through YMI). Support comes from MBMSI budget.

Singe-term Missionaries CorePlus – Programs of single terms of service or shorter terms of service of nine months or more. Support is through personal fundraising.

TREK – A program dedicated to developing young leaders. After two months of intense training, the participants embark on a four to eight month foray into serious ministry in North America and/or other countries.

Acronymns

CPE – Church Partner Evangelism

MB – Mennonite Brethren

MBBS – Mennonite Brethren Biblical Seminary

MBMSI – Mennonite Brethren Mission and Service International

MBY – Mennonite Brethren Youth

YMI – Youth Mission International

Mennonite Brethren Resources

A Pilgrimage of Faith
The Mennonite Brethren Church in Russia and North America
1860 - 1990
J. B. Toews

A thorough look at the theological underpinnings of the Mennonite Brethren Church. It is a backward glance to see how we have done and how we are doing. It is a call to reflection, spiritual awareness and ultimately to repentance and renewal.

$14.99 CDN $11.99 US

Confession of Faith of the United States and Canadian Mennonite Brethren Churches
Complete text of the 18 articles that not only describe how the Mennonite Brethren Church in Canada and the United States interpret the Bible but is also an authoritative guide for biblical interpretation, theological identity and ethical practices. Each article has accompanying biblical references that serve primarily as proof-texts for the article.

$1.50 CDN $1.00 US

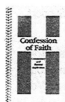

Commentary and Pastoral Application for the Confession of Faith
Each of the 18 articles is reprinted in this book, followed by commentary to present the biblical background and a pastoral application to discuss implementation of the article in the life of the church. The book is intended for leaders, members and inquirers.

$9.99 CDN $7.99 US

Other Supplementary Resources
Sidewalk Version
A brief introductory of MB beliefs and distinctives in pamphlet form
Sold in groups of 50
$4.00 CDN $3.00 US

Liturgical Version
Uses Scripture and contemporary language to make the confession available to the congregation for worship. Available in two formats.

Transparency Masters   Booklet
$5.00 CDN $3.50 US $3.50 CDN $2.50 US

Order Information:
Toll Free Order Line: 1-800-545-7322 U.S. and Canada
Email: custserv@kindredproductions.com
Web site: www.kindredproductions.com
Fax: 204-654-1865 Canada   620-947-3226 US